UPSIDE DOWN

Nothing on the Clock

The RAF Benevolent Fund Book of After Dinner Stories

EDITED BY:
Group Captain J.K. Walters
Flight Lieutenant A.M. Bryne
Sergeant P.T. Gallichan
Sergeant M.R. James

Woodfield

First published in paperback in 1991 by

WOODFIELD PUBLISHING
Woodfield House, Arundel Road, Fontwell,
West Sussex BN18 0SD, England.

© Group Captain J.K. Walters, 1990

A catalogue record of this book
is available from the British Library

ISBN 1 – 873203 – 26 – 8

Printed in Great Britain

FOREWORD

by Air Chief Marshal Sir Thomas Kennedy GCB AFC DL
Controller, Royal Air Force Benevolent Fund

Throughout history, one of the enduring qualities of the British Serviceman has been his keen sense of humour. Irrespective of his situation or personal circumstances, has invariably been able to find something to raise a smile or cause a chuckle. He is a master of repartee and the pithy observation.

This is an integral part of his make-up and is manifested at almost every military reunion that takes place. These gatherings follow a fairly standard pattern – very noisy stories which get taller by the hour, and a great deal of laughter. Much of the reminiscing is based on personal experiences and is usually expounded with a refreshing degree of self-denigration.

The Serviceman loves to puncture the pompous or deflate the stuffy, and he has a healthy disregard for all forms of authority. Long may this state of affairs continue. I thoroughly commend this small volume to all serving and ex-Servicemen and women wherever they are. Buying this book will help the Royal Air Force Benevolent Fund because, 10 percent of the cover price will come to support our Appeal for £20 million to enable us to continue the work we have been doing for the past 71 years, ever since the inception of the Fund in 1919, i.e. to relieve distress amongst past and present members of the Royal Air Force and their dependants.

Nicholson, VC of RAF Church Fenton. The only Battle of Britain fighter pilot to be awarded the Victoria Cross.

INTRODUCTION

The idea of this book had been at the back of my mind for some years, but it was the RAF Benevolent Fund's 'Reach for the Sky' appeal that finally provided the impetus to get it off the stocks. The appeal was linked to the 50th anniversary of the Battle of Britain and, as an officer from RAF Church Fenton won the only VC awarded to Fighter Command during the Second World War, it seemed appropriate that Church Fenton should come up with something special to help the appeal.

We trawled the whole of the RAF (and everyone outside that we could think of) for contributions. The response, frankly, overwhelmed the editorial committee: over 800 stories were submitted.

From those 800 odd stories, we have selected the 151 that made us laugh the most and were considered printable. As far as the boundaries of good taste were concerned, we set our lower limit as the material that we felt we could tell to a liberated mother-in-law; but only just! If the material in this book oversteps your particular mark, we can only apologise.

The committee are immensely grateful to all those contributors who donated stories. I should also like to express particular thanks to four officers who trawled, on our behalf, those places that we did not know how to (or did not dare) reach. Air Commodore Peter Gover covered the whole of RAF Germany, and a lot of other places on the Continent that we would never have thought of; Group Captain Ian Junor did the same for the Air Secretary's department; Air Commodore Nigel Baldwin persuaded most of Headquarters Strike Command to come up with something; and Group Captain Philip

Sturley covered all of the great and famous at the Ministry of Defence.

Finally, most heartfelt thanks to some special helpers. Jack Aspinwall MP, whose own books of this nature have long been my staple reference for public speaking, readily volunteered to act in an advisory capacity and has kept us clear of many Pooh traps. Margaret Beaumont, my typist, did extra typing in her own time, and also painted the picture of Nicholson VC which appeared on the back cover of the first edition. Flying Officer Steve Dean found time in a busy and demanding Flying Training course to produce the cartoon for the frontispiece.

The original hardback edition published by Woodfield, was funded privately by RAF Church Fenton. There was no serious financial risk involved because a considerable number of RAF personnel had pledged to underwrite any losses on the project. Additionally, a number of commercial firms paid for advertising space which covered the production costs.

The original underwriters and advertises will not see themselves mentioned herein, but the editorial committee and the RAF Benevolent Fund are immensely grateful for their support, without which the original book would never have seen the light of day.

Similarly we are grateful to Woodfield Publishing for taking the commercial risk of producing this paperback edition and for agreeing to pay 10% of the cover price to the RAF Benevolent Fund.

JKW
RAF Church Fenton
June 1991

UPSIDE DOWN . . .

The beautiful young female medical student was stunned when the Professor asked her:

"What part of the human body enlarges to about ten times its normal size during periods of excitement and emotion?"

"I refuse to answer that question," stammered the girl, blushing and avoiding the looks and giggles of her male classmates. One of these was called upon next and answered correctly:

"The pupil of the eye."

"Well done," said the Professor; "as for you, Miss Rogers, your refusal to answer the question makes three things apparent: firstly, you did not do last night's homework; secondly, you have a dirty mind; and thirdly, marriage is likely to be a great disappointment to you!"

Air Commodore D.J. Loveridge, OBE FBIM
Ministry of Defence

The late Air Chief Marshal Sir John Stacey was well known in the Royal Air Force for his appetite for flying. He was much respected for a clear affinity with his crews and for his concern for their interests. He was also, on occasion, guilty of recounting his experiences as a pilot at some length ... but aren't we all!

In the late 1970s he was Commander-in-Chief Royal Air Force Germany and Commander of the Second Allied Tactical Air Force. One evening he was bidden to speak after dinner in the Officers' Mess at the RAF Hospital at Wegberg. He did so fresh from a Phantom sortie with the Luftwaffe Richthofen Wing, which had ended in a sporting approach and landing in a strong and blustery crosswind. In the course of his speech, he was 'entertaining' his audience to a blow by blow account of his victory over the elements, seemingly oblivious to the general lack of interest that the tale aroused in this particular gathering. Suddenly from the end of the table, the *sotto voce* aside of a junior surgeon summed up the reaction of the party:

"Nothing to it, old boy – just like doing a vasectomy with two left gloves on!"

Air Vice Marshal A.F.C. Hunter, CBE AFC MA LLB
Commandant, Royal Air Force Staff College

☆ ☆ ☆

An Irishman went into the confessional.

"Forgive me father, for I have sinned; I had intercourse with my wife yesterday."

"That is not a sin, my son," said the priest; "God put men and women on this earth to procreate the human race in that way. Intercourse between man and wife, within the sanctity of holy matrimony, is far from being a sin; it is actually encouraged by the Church."

"But you don't understand, Father," replied the man. "I was unkind to my wife; I took her by surprise; she was just bending over the freezer to get out a chicken when I came up behind her and grabbed her. Despite her struggles, I had my way. That was not very nice, was it?"

"Well, my son," said the priest, "I agree that it could be presented as a little on the unkind side. On the other hand, when a man and a woman have been married for a long time, they sometimes find it helpful to introduce a little variety into their lovemaking. Provided that you did not hurt or injure your

UPSIDE DOWN . . .

wife, I find it difficult to view your actions as sinful. However, it is obviously troubling you, so I suggest that you go into the body of the church and say three Hail Marys; that can be an end of the matter."

"Oh. So I am not banned from the church then, Father?"

"Of course not, my son; how ridiculous. Whatever gave you that idea?"

"Well... it's just that we were in Sainsbury's when it happened."

Group Captain J.K. Walters
Commanding Officer, RAF Church Fenton

☆ ☆ ☆

Three nuns were driving in the Convent's Mini-Metro when they were unfortunately involved in a head-on collision with a juggernaut lorry. Not surprisingly they were all killed instantly, and proceeded to Heaven.

When they arrived at the Pearly Gates they were confident of a swift admission to Paradise; however they were met by a rather officious St Peter who announced that, regardless of how good they had been or who they were, they could not be admitted without taking a test.

The nuns were a little put out but, having no option, agreed to take the test; the first one stepped forward and stood in front of St Peter.

"Right..." said St Peter, "...what was the name of the first man?"

"Adam" replied the first nun instantly.

"Correct" said St Peter. Immediately the gates of Heaven burst open, sunlight came streaming through and the attending angels blew a fanfare on their trumpets. With her head held high, the first nun strode into Paradise and the gates slammed shut behind her.

"OK," said St Peter, "who's next?"

"Me" said the second nun timidly, stepping forward to stand in front of the Saint.

"Very well; tell me the name of the first woman" demanded St Peter. A long and uncomfortable silence ensued. Just when it seemed that she would fail to answer, the second nun's eyes lit up.

"It was Eve" she cried.

"Spot on" said St Peter; and the gates of Heaven flew open, sunlight streamed forth and the angels blew a fanfare. The second nun strode proudly in through the gates and they closed behind her.

The third nun stepped forward.

"What did the first woman say to the first man?" asked St Peter.

The nun shuffled her feet and tugged nervously at her habit, racking her brains for an answer; the silence seemed interminable.

"M-m-my word" she stammered; "that *is* a hard one."

The gates of Heaven burst open, sunlight streamed through and the attending angels blew a fanfare on their trumpets...

Wing Commander T.J. Gerrard, BA ACIS MBIM
Headquarters Strike Command

At the Battle of Waterloo, Colonel Clement, an infantry commander, fought with the most conspicuous bravery but, unfortunately, was shot through the head. Napoleon, hearing of his gallantry and misfortune, gave instructions for him to be carried into a farm where Larrey, the Surgeon General, was operating.

One glance convinced Larrey that Clement's situation was critical so, taking up a saw, he removed the top of the skull and placed the brains on the operating table. At that moment an aide-de-camp rushed into the room shouting "Is General Clement here?"

Clement, on hearing this, sat up and exclaimed: "No! but *Colonel* Clement is."

"Oh, mon General," cried the aide-de-camp, embracing him, "the Emperor was overwhelmed when we heard of your gallantry that he has promoted you on the field of battle to the rank of General."

Clement rubbed his eyes, got off the table, clapped the top of his skull on his head and made to leave.

"Mon General ... your brains!" shouted Larrey after him.

Still accelerating away, the gallant Frenchman shouted back:

"Tiens; now that I am a General, I shall no longer require them!"

Air Commodore N.B. Baldwin
Air Commodore Plans, Headquarters Strike Command

A hoary old Flight Lieutenant Navigator, whose flying exploits were all behind him, had been despatched to a recruiting booth in a seaside town for the duration of a military Tattoo. For days he patiently endured the questions of all the young people who visited his stand. Much to his disappointment, all of them wanted to be pilots; whenever he explained the thrills of air navigation and touched on his own many daring deeds, they invariably wandered away looking bored.

On the last day, a scruffy looking youth wandered up to the stand and sneered "Got any good jobs going, mate?; I've half a mind to become a pilot."

"We certainly have, son..." replied the Navigator, "...and it sounds as if you are eminently well qualified. Sign here!"

Squadron Leader J.M. Clifford, BSc
NAMMA, Munich

As a young junior officer I was part of the team manning the RAF stand at the Radio Show at Earls Court in 1960. Here I was given an early experience of the total loss of authority which can be engendered by the Serviceman's wit.

"Has Squadron Leader Wright brought up the oscilloscope yet?" I enquired of the Corporal.

"I am sorry, Sir," was the reply, "I did not realise that he had swallowed it!"

Air Marshal Sir John Kemball, CBE
Chief of Staff, Headquarters Strike Command

A young couple went into a shop to buy a washing machine and were approached by a keen salesman. "How can I help you?" he enquired.

"We are looking for a washing machine," replied the wife; "it must be the very best that you have, regardless of cost."

"Certainly Madam," replied the salesman; "this German machine here is probably ideal for you. Although it is expensive, it does absolutely everything for you and is simplicity itself to operate. All you so is lift the lid, put in the washing and detergent, close the lid and turn it on. It fills itself with water at exactly the right temperature; it does a biological prewash; a main wash; it then spins at 2000 revolutions per minute until the washing is virtually dry. Finally an automatic tumble drying sequence cuts in and takes the last traces of moisture out of the material.In only 25 minutes, your washing ends up like new."

"Very good," said the husband, "but what about really dirty nappies?"

"No problem at all," said the salesman. He went through his entire sales patter again, ending up with "...and in only 25 minutes the *really* dirty nappies come out looking just like brand new Harringtons Squares."

"I see," said the husband, "so all I have to do is lift the lid, put in the really dirty nappies and some detergent, and turn it on, and in 25 minutes they come out like new?"

"No Sir," said the salesman, "you forgot to close the lid. All you would get would be a face full of sh★★."

MORAL: Always obey technical orders to the letter.

Group Captain (Retired) John McDonald
Associated Aircraft

☆ ☆ ☆

Some years ago, when we had Royal Air Force Flying Training Schools in Northern Ireland, a student and his instructor took off from Royal Air Force Bishops Court in a Tiger Moth, the two-seater training aircraft of the day. Unfortunately at some stage they lost control of the aircraft, which crashed into a cemetery near a small Irish town, killing both occupants.

The local authorities had the sad task of clearing up after the accident. Their activities were duly recorded in the local newspaper:

> "The authorities are still sifting through the debris from the aircraft crash in the town cemetery last Thursday. So far they have recovered 423 bodies."

Air Marshal Sir Michael Simmons, KCB AFC
Deputy Controller, Aircraft; MOD Procurement Executive

One tradition which the Royal Air Force has taken from its sister Services is the importance of treating a squadron standard with due respect. It was therefore a matter of great concern when the squadron standard bearer, on collecting the standard from the locked storage room in the Officers' Mess at RAF Laarbruch (in Germany), discovered that the top section of the orb and eagle at the tip of the standard staff had snapped off.

The squadron commander convened a formal enquiry and evidence was taken on oath. The broken section was labelled as "Exhibit A" and after the due processes of Air Force Law, the junior officer standard bearer was found to blame.

It then fell to me, as squadron adjutant, to arrange for the necessary repairs to be carried out. Happily, there was a local German jeweller whom I knew did metalwork, as he always engraved our squadron tankards. Communication was easy, despite the lack of a common language, and the standard was left for repair.

The following week, it was ready for collection; I admired the seamless weld which he had polished so that it could not be detected. Then I caught the glint of the faultlessly engraved gothic script around the orb:

EXHIBIT A

I suddenly remembered how we had always communicated the wording for our tankard inscriptions ... there seemed little doubt about who would be at the receiving end of the next Unit Inquiry!

Air Commodore T. Garden, MA MPhil
Director, Air Force Staff Duties, Ministry of Defence

☆ ☆ ☆

A veterinary surgeon was telephoned late at night by a distraught woman:

"Please come quickly; my two dogs are stuck together and I don't know what to do; and the male one seems to be in some considerable pain."

"Try throwing a bucket of cold water over them," said the vet, not very pleased at being thus disturbed.

"I've already tried that," sobbed the woman "and it didn't work."

"Then hit them both with the biggest stick you can find; that should do the trick ."

"I have; and it didn't work."

"I'll tell you what to do," said the vet "replace your telephone and I'll call you back."

"Oh. Do you think that the ringing of the telephone will cause my dogs to separate, then?"

"I can't actually promise it," snarled the vet "but it has certainly just worked for me!"

Air Commodore R. Chapple, MB BS MFCM MFOM MBIM MRCS LPCP DPH
RAF Hospital, Wroughton

☆ ☆ ☆

At RAF Leeming some years ago, a WRAF officer wrote the following in the Officers' Mess suggestions book:

"Perhaps I have a vivid imagination, but the male officers frequently return to the bar from the toilet and then use their hands to take ice from the ice bucket. In the interests of hygiene, could the Mess please provide tongs?"

The reply from the President of the Mess Committee read:

"Thank you for your suggestion. Tongs will be provided in the gentlemen's toilet."

Squadron Leader (retired) M.J. Fletcher
RAF Linton-on-Ouse

☆ ☆ ☆

Today we accept opinion polls as an everyday part of our lives – GALLUP and MORI regularly canvas views on a whole variety of topics. However, in the early days of such polls, the system was not always quite so readily understood. In one of their very first polls, GALLUP asked a number of companies in a particular area to list the total number of employees on their books, broken down by sex.

One company replied that although none of their employees were actually broken down by sex, a few of them did have a bit of a drink problem!

Group Captain R.W. Bryden
Headquarters Royal Air Force Germany

☆ ☆ ☆

Anyone who has ever had anything to do with Electronic Warfare will know that the subject is complex and constantly changing, so it becomes of paramount importance to attend courses, quite often abroad, to keep abreast of developments and new technology. Unfortunately this laudable motivation for absence on courses is not always appreciated by our loved ones, who are invariably left behind on these occasions.

I should also explain that, over the years, a Crow has come to be adopted as the emblem associated with Electronic Warfare; so much so that "The Association of Old Crows" is now a very successful international organisation for people interested in the subject. Quite how a crow came to be associated with Electronic Warfare Officers (EWO) has never been explained to my satisfaction, although unkind outsiders (usually pilots) will claim that it is because EWOs squawk a lot, defecate a lot, and one has to throw stones at them to get them to fly!

My story concerns an officer who was preparing to depart for an Electronic Warfare convention abroad; his wife observed that he was packing a fancy dress costume in the shape of a giant crow. Naturally, she was somewhat suspicious, but he explained that on the penultimate evening of the convention there would be a fancy-dress social evening; because of his connection with Electronic Warfare, he felt it wholly appropriate to go in the guise of a giant crow.

The wife appeared to accept the explanation, but was determined to find out for herself just what happens on such occasions. Unbeknown to the officer, the good lady acquired herself a costume that rendered her unrecognisable and journeyed independently to the convention centre. She somehow managed to gain admission to the social event.

Needless to say, she had no difficulty in finding the giant crow and, determined to put her husband to the test, she approached it, disguised her voice, and engaged him in provocative conversation. The response was immediate and fulsome, and this made her even more determined to carry on. She allowed herself to be taken back to his room for the night, taking great care not to remove her mask before the light was out. Next morning she arose while it was still dark, and left for home to await her husband's return.

The next day the luckless officer returned home to be greeted by a smiling wife – but what a smile!

"How was the convention?" she asked, preparing to go for the kill.

"Just fine," he replied "until the evening of the social function."

"What happened then?" she enquired suspiciously.

"Well I developed the most awful cold, and couldn't face going. However, all was not lost, for I was able to lend my fancy dress to one of the other officers – he, apparently, had a whale of a time!"

Squadron Leader J. Gilbert
RAF Spadeadam

The Chief of an American Indian tribe in the early part of this century was an enlightened man; he saw that the future lay in technology, and he persuaded his people to put all their savings into a fund so that his eldest son could go to University, become an electrical engineer, and bring honour and prosperity to the tribe.

The Chief's son went to University and did well; he returned to the tribe three years later with a good upper second and a strong wish to repay the tribe for their faith in him. He thought long and hard about how he might best do this, and finally decided that a practical and beneficial application of his electrical engineering knowledge would be the most appropriate way of showing his gratitude. So for several days he could be seen and heard about the camp, putting up poles and stringing wire about the place; sawing and hammering and doing all the things electrical engineers love to do. Finally he announced that he had finished.

His proud father, the Chief, called the tribe together to see what his son had done for them. The son stood up; he thanked the tribe for their faith in him and explained how he had decided to repay them.

"I thought back to my youth in the camp," he said "and I tried to remember what the most miserable thing about it was. And I decided that it must surely be getting up in the middle of the night, leaving my nice warm bed in our nice warm tepee, and having to find my way down the dark and uneven path to the dark little tepee down by the river. So I have designed and made a lighting system for the path and the little tepee." And he pressed the switch, and lights illuminated on poles all down the path and inside the little tepee.

And the Chief said "My son has truly repaid our investment in him; for not only is he the first member of the tribe to go to University, but he is also the first Indian in history to wire a head for a reservation."

Air Vice Marshal J.P.R. Browne, CBE BSc(Eng) CEng MICE MRAeS MBIM
Ministry of Defence

☆ ☆ ☆

A Tactical Supply Wing (TSW) junior officer, after many years spent on detachments enjoying the delights of local hospitality all over the world, was in a very grave condition. He had contracted various diseases, some sexually transmitted, some brought on by excesses of every imaginable kind, and was now paying the price.

Such was the gravity of the situation that his mother was shipped in from home and a priest was called to administer the last rites; the Station Medical Officer at RAF Stafford was even prepared to give him a sick note – albeit to be reviewed daily.

The mother arrived at the Station Medical Centre, trying desperately hard to maintain self control, but clearly in a state of some distress. She demanded more details of her son's condition.

"I am afraid" replied the embarrassed Medical Officer, "that your son has Venereal Disease, Non Specific Urethritis, Herpes, AIDS and cirrhosis of the liver; the prognosis is not good."

"What treatment are you giving him?" asked the mother.

"Well, we have him on a diet of flapjacks, japetes, pizzas and omelettes," replied the doctor.

"Will that cure him?"

"Sadly I don't think so," sighed the Medical Officer; "they are just the only things that we can push under the door."

Squadron Leader D.S. Belmore, MInstPS
Tactical Supply Wing, RAF Stafford

☆ ☆ ☆

Excerpt from The Yorkshire Post

The man was charged with driving under the influence of alcohol and will appear in court tomorrow. He has been before the magistrates on similar charges on many previous occasions. As a consequence he has received intensive treatment for alcoholism at a variety of corrective institutions.

When apprehended and cautioned, the defendant claimed that his actions had been entirely innocent; he had recently been discharged, declared fit, from a local "drying out" establishment.

"All I did" he stated "was to have a couple of drinks to see if I was cured."

Squadron Leader R.A. Bealer
Headquarters Strike Command

☆ ☆ ☆

During the Kuwait crisis in 1961, the British military presence in the Middle East was increased by reinforcements from the United Kingdom. The air deployment route to Aden included a particularly long sector over almost featureless terrain from

El Adem in Libya to Khartoum. The requirement to avoid Egyptian airspace posed an additional problem for aircraft with limited fuel reserves. This led some crews to take a short cut across the infamous "Nasser's Corner" in an attempt to arrive at the destination with sufficient fuel at least to taxi clear of the runway at their destination.

After a Canberra pilot had decided that prudence necessitated this course of action his navigator announced that, in addition to the fuel problem, he was also short of position fixes and would welcome details of any features visible on the ground. Eventually the pilot told the navigator that the aircraft was about to overfly a group of pyramids. The navigator peered out of the cockpit window and tried to orientate his topographical chart with the ground.

"It's no good," he said to the pilot with a note of disappointment in his voice, "it must be an old map – they are not marked."

Squadron Leader M.P. Westwood
Headquarters Strike Command

An Education Officer, new to the RAF and whose academic qualifications were all on the Arts side, found to his horror that his job entailed giving scientific lessons to airmen as part of the general education scheme.

On the first morning he delivered a physics lecture, during which he held up a glass of water; he announced that water froze at zero degrees Centigrade and boiled at 90 degrees. An airman put up his hand and challenged the statement, saying that he had been taught at school that water boiled at 100 degrees Centigrade. The lecturer rebuked him, claiming that the book said 90 degrees.

The following morning the lecturer offered an apology to the airman concerned:

"I'm sorry," he said, "I turned over two pages at once; it's a right angle that boils at 90 degrees."

Group Captain J.M. Walker
RAF Carlisle

☆ ☆ ☆

There had been a bit of an affray in the Airmen's Club on Saturday night and on Monday morning, a Squadron Leader was hearing the charges against those involved.

One of the witnesses was the RAF Police Corporal who had been called to the club and had arrested those involved. After hearing his evidence, the Squadron Leader said to him:

"And I understand that you were kicked in the fracas?"

"No Sir," said the policeman, "I was kicked in the stomach, just above the fracas."

Flight Lieutenant (Retired) D.C. Williams

☆ ☆ ☆

A snake and a rabbit were going in opposite directions along a narrow trail in the jungle and bumped into each other.

"Hello," said the snake, "what are you?"

"I don't know," said the rabbit, "I am blind and I have never been able to see myself. What are you?"

"Well, I am blind too, so I don't know either;" said the snake "but I have an idea. Let us feel each other all over; then we will be able to tell each other what we are."

"OK," said the rabbit, "you go first."

The snake began his inspection. "Well, you've got two big floppy ears ... big buck teeth ... fur all over ... and a little bob tail; I think you must be a rabbit."

"Thank you." said the rabbit, and started to feel over the snake. "Right; you've got large staring eyes ... fangs ... a forked tongue ... a long slimy body ... and no balls. I reckon you're a lawyer."

Squadron Leader P.R. Hunter
Ministry of Defence

☆ ☆ ☆

A young Australian undergraduate obtained a vacation job doing behavioural research for the University of Sydney. The University authorities wanted to compare the sexual habits of young Australians with the earlier findings of the Kinsey Report in America.

He worked his way along Bondi Beach one sunny Saturday afternoon in high summer, carrying a clipboard and interviewing all the young males on the beach. Towards the end of the afternoon he approached yet another archetypal surfer – a bronzed, muscular young man with long blond hair and with a surf board by his side.

"Excuse me, sport," said the researcher, "I am carrying out a survey of sexual behaviour and I wonder if you'd mind if I asked you some intimate and personal questions?"

"Not at all, mate," replied the young Adonis, "go ahead."

"Right-oh," said the researcher; "firstly, I'd like you to estimate, roughly, what your 'scoring' rate is with women – say per week."

"Well now," mused the surfer, "I'll have to think about that... Now let me see... I suppose, if we averaged it over, say, a year... my mean rate would be... about one point two times a week."

"I see," said the undergraduate, scribbling on his clipboard. "Now, I hope you don't mind if I get even more personal. You see, I have interviewed literally hundreds of young men on this survey, and yours is by far the lowest estimate that I have yet come across. Would you care to comment?"

"Not really," said the other; "I reckon I'm doing pretty well for a Catholic priest with no car!"

Group Captain J.K. Walters
Commanding Officer, RAF Church Fenton

☆ ☆ ☆

In connection with a major anniversary of the Battle of Britain, the television chat show host had gathered together a selection of foreigners who had taken part; they included a Frenchman from the Free French Air Force, a Dutchman, a Pole and a Czech. All had very distinguished war records, and each was asked in turn about some of their exploits.

When the Pole's turn came the host remarked that, of all those present, this man seemed to have won the most awards for gallantry. "I noticed particularly" said the host "that you had been awarded the DSO; a very rare honour – could you tell us how that came about?"

"Vell," said the Pole, "it vos like dis. I vos leading a section of Shpitfires on patrol over de Channel; ve vos at fifteen t'ousand feet in de Manston Sector ven suddenly my vingman shouts "Fokkers in de sun!" and I look up and sure enough dere vos t'ree Fokkers diving down towards us."

"So," interrupted the host hurriedly, "you were attacked by a flight of Focke-Wolfe 190 German fighter aircraft."

"No," said the Pole, "dey vos flying Messerschmidt 109s."

Anon

☆ ☆ ☆

Standing here to speak to you tonight reminds me of an occasion when I gave a speech to a Sixth Form ladies college. The headmistress approached me beforehand and, realising that I was fairly new to public speaking, said "ABC my boy!"

"Sorry?" I replied.

"ABC ... Always Be Convivial, and you'll go down well."

So when I stood up I thought "ABC"... and it worked! The girls were hushed at first, but gradually they loosened up and, by the time I sat down, they were roaring with laughter. The headmistress approached me afterwards.

"Not bad, eh?" I enthused. "I remembered ABC and they loved me!"

"Mmm. Yes." she murmured. Perhaps you should have remembered another piece of advice: XYZ."

"XYZ?" I queried.

She explained:

"Before standing to speak, eXamine Your Zip!"

Flight Lieutenant S. Phelps-Jones, BA
Universities of Glasgow and Strathclyde Air Squadron

☆ ☆ ☆

The pilot training system has its lighter moments. There is the story of the student pilot being given his monthly "Emergencies Quiz" by his instructor.

"You have a Hydraulics Failure caption, no brake pressure and a smell of burning" said the instructor. "What would you do?"

"I think, Sir," replied the student "that I would already have done it!"

Squadron Leader (Retired) M.J. Fletcher
RAF Linton-on-Ouse

☆ ☆ ☆

Two old school friends – James and Clive – meet by accident in a local street after not having seen one another for several years. James is looking very prosperous, whilst Clive is rather down at heel.

"Well James," says Clive, "how's things?"

"Can't complain," says James; "how about you?"

"Oh, not so bad," says Clive; "are you married?"

"Yes indeed," says James. "Do you remember Fiona Crumpington-Smythe? Well I married her and we have got three lovely children."

"Still at school, are they?" says Clive.

"Well," says James, "my elder son is now at Oxford, reading Medicine; my daughter is at a finishing school in Switzerland; and my younger son is in his last term at Eton."

"Oh," says Clive; "got a car?"

"Yes indeed," says James. "That's my Rolls Royce parked over there; Fiona has a Volvo estate and the kids have their own runabouts – Escorts, Metros, that sort of thing."

"Live near here?" asks Clive.

"We were very lucky," says James; "we found this lovely place just outside Harrogate; not too big – only 7 bedrooms; old vicarage, actually – but it does have a paddock where the kids can keep their hunters."

"Dear me," says Clive, "you must have a very good job."

"Yes I do," says James. "As a matter of fact I'm in shipping. I work fer Cunard..."

"I work bloody hard too," says Clive, "but I'm not in your league."

Air Commodore M.P. Crotty, MSc BA(Hons)
Director Support Management 3 (RAF)

☆ ☆ ☆

Some years ago, my pilot and I had occasion to depart rather suddenly from our Phantom. Having ejected safely, we both landed uncomfortably from our parachute descents – my pilot sustained a fracture to his spine and I had a broken leg. After a short hospitalisation in Scotland where the accident occurred, we were both flown south to a Royal Air Force hospital to continue our recovery.

On arrival at the hospital late in the evening, we were given temporary accommodation in a small side ward. The following morning, I was taken up to a new ward in a wheelchair; however, my pilot had to be moved up in his bed as a consequence of his back injury. Thus I was taken up first and, on arriving at the small ward, was placed in one of the two beds; the other was being removed to make way for my colleague.

As I was settling down and awaiting his arrival, a young nurse came into the ward. She picked up the clipboard from the end of my bed and started to take down my personal details. On hearing my rank, name and unit she exclaimed: "Oh; you're the one who ejaculated!" Realising her mistake, the embarrassed young girl fled from the ward and a few minutes later my colleague was wheeled in to find me convulsed with laughter. When the medical orderlies had left, he asked me why I was laughing; I explained, and he then himself dissolved into fits of laughter which caused him some pain owing to his injuries.

Just as the laughter had subsided and the ward had returned to normal, the young nurse reappeared. Studiously ignoring me, she made her way to the other side of the ward and picked up the clipboard at the bottom of my pilot's bed.

"Rank?" she asked.

"Flight Lieutenant."

"Name, unit?"

He gave them.

"Oh!" she exclaimed once again, "you're the other one who ej.. ej.. ej... baled out, aren't you?"

Wing Commander A.D. Moir, BSc MRIN
Commanding Officer, No 43(F) Squadron

☆ ☆ ☆

Once upon a time, in a hot arid country, there dwelt a sensitive young man. It was "mule" country, and they were not short of the particular trait of their breed – stubbornness.

Our sensitive young man owned one of these animals, and this caused something of a conflict. He could not bring himself to beat it in the traditional way in order to get it to obey. There was much cajoling and enticing – he was even reduced, now and again, to picking up the mule's feet, one at a time, and moving them forward in order to make any progress at all.

One day, as they were making their painful progress along some hot and dusty street, our sensitive soul saw a notice:

MULES TRAINED BY KINDNESS AND PERSUASION

This seemed like the answer to all his prayers, for he really was at the end of his tether with his stubborn beast.

He entered the courtyard to be greeted by the "Trainer", who confirmed that he did indeed train mules using only kindness and persuasion. Our sensitive soul duly handed over his animal and retired to the shade to observe the training. Imagine his horror when he saw the "Trainer" advance on his mule with an enormous wooden club which, with a mighty swing, he brought down cracking on the animal's head.

The mule staggered around with its front legs getting further and further apart. The sensitive young man was distraught; he rushed over to the trainer and started beating at his chest.

"I thought you said that you trained using only kindness and persuasion?"

"Ah, yes," replied the trainer, "but first you have to attract their attention!"

Squadron Leader D. Berry
RAF Lyneham

☆ ☆ ☆

A WRNS officer was visiting a Scottish Army unit in Edinburgh and staying in their Officers' Mess. Returning to her room one night, she saw an officer asleep in the ante-room, obviously the worse for drink. Having long been fascinated by the mystique of what, if anything, Scotsmen wore under the kilt, she decided that this was too good an opportunity to miss; she gently lifted his kilt and satisfied her curiosity. As this had not disturbed him at all, her mischievous nature got the better of her; she removed a red ribbon from her hair and tied a bow under the unsuspecting officer's kilt.

In the morning "Jock" was awakened by his steward; he could not remember anything about his activities of the previous evening, or even how he had managed to get back to his room and arrive, fully dressed, on his own bed. He rose, groaning, undressed and made his way to the shower room. As he entered, he saw himself in the mirror and caught sight of the offending ribbon. He scratched his head, furrowed his brow, and thought long and hard about how he could possibly have found himself in this condition. Eventually he gave up the struggle; throwing his towel over his shoulder he strode off to the shower cubicle exclaiming:

"Well, laddie, I don't know where we ended up last night; but it's good to see that we won first prize!"

Squadron Leader D.B. Dunsmuir, DPhysEd
RAF Turnhouse

☆ ☆ ☆

An extremely wealthy German businessman drove his top-of-the-line Mercedes off the Fishguard to Rosslare ferry and set off for a touring holiday in Ireland. Shortly after leaving the town, he was cruising along, enjoying the scenery and remarking to himself on the very low traffic density, when he espied a figure ahead thumbing a lift.

He pulled up beside the hitch-hiker who proved to be a spritely 50 year old Irish tramp – classically dressed in a collarless shirt, complete with stud, and a baggy pair of trousers tucked into a pair of wellington boots.

"Shur, 'tis a beautiful motor-car you've got here and no mistake," said the little Irishman, settling into the passenger seat.

"Ja," said the German proudly, "Zis is a Mercedes."

"Oy see," said the other, "but what is dat funny little ting like a steering wheel on de front of de bonnet for?"

"What an idiot," thought the German "we have a right one here." So, deciding to play it for all it was worth, he said:

"Zat is mein aiming sight; I get to score ze points for each pedestrian zat I knock over – Ja?" So saying, he pointed up the long hill they were climbing and said: "See, here is one." He was indicating another tramp, similarly attired to his passenger, and hitching a ride in the other direction from the opposite side of the road.

"Vatch zis," said the German; and the Mercedes lurched forward under full throttle, straight at the figure at the side of the road. The tramp went rigid in the passenger seat, eyes like organ stops. At the very last minute, the German spun the wheel to the left so as just to miss the pedestrian and return the Mercedes to the correct side of the road. To his horror, there was a loud clunk and, looking in the rear view mirror, he saw a tumbling figure sailing through the air.

"Gott in Himmel!" cried the German, "I thought zat I had just missed him."

"Ah now, never fear sorr," said the little Irishman, "shur ye would have done, but didn't Oy get him wit de door!"

Group Captain J.L. Uprichard
Ministry of Defence

☆ ☆ ☆

A sloth who lived in a rough part of town was walking home late one night when he was mugged by two snails. Later, at the police station where he had reported the offence, he was asked by an Inspector if he would be able to recognise his assailants if he saw them again. After an interminable pause he replied:

"Er, I don't think so, officer; it all happened too quickly"

Wing Commander J.R. Whitston
Commanding Officer, RAF Manston

☆ ☆ ☆

During a lecture on Scientific Progress in the Twentieth Century, the eminent lecturer asked a selection of officers what they considered to be the most significant development of the century.

The airman replied: "The jet engine which has not only revolutionised civil aviation, but has changed military thinking and tactics out of all recognition."

The answer from the submariner was: "The invention of nuclear power which has enabled the oceans to be exploited more fully from a military point of view and has turned submarines into the capital ships of the future."

The RAF Regiment officer's suggestion was, however, of a more mundane nature:

"The Thermos flask," he said, "because it keeps hot things hot and cold things cold."

Not overly impressed with this suggestion, the lecturer asked him to explain why he thought the humble Thermos flask was so wonderful.

"Well," replied the 'Rockape', "how does it know the difference?"

Wing Commander M. Harwood-Grayson, MA RAF
Ministry of Defence

☆ ☆ ☆

An old Arab sheik, who was an extremely keen golfer, sent
his son to Britain to purchase a set of golf clubs for him. When
the son had been away for four weeks the father, worried about
him, asked his London embassy to try and track him down.
The embassy located the young man in Scotland and told him
to telephone his father. This he duly did, apologising for the
delay and explaining that he had bought most of the clubs; but
he was having difficulty with the last two as neither Gleneagles
nor St Andrews would sell.

Flight Lieutenant E.A. Dulake, WRAF
Ministry of Defence.

☆ ☆ ☆

Four gentlemen found themselves sharing a carriage on a long
train journey. One thought it would be a good idea to start a
conversation:

"It looks as though we shall be travelling together for
some time, so perhaps we should introduce ourselves: I'm John
Smith, a Squadron Leader in the Royal Air Force. I'm married
and I have 3 children, one still at school, one at university and
one training to be a solicitor."

"That's extraordinary," said the second, "because I'm
also a Squadron Leader in the Royal Air Force, and I'm also
married with 3 children – two still at school and the third at
university studying to be a doctor."

"Well, you'll never believe this," chipped in the third,
"but I'm also a Squadron Leader in the Royal Air Force.

I'm also married, and also have 3 children – one at school, one training to be an accountant, and the third a qualified surveyor."

They all turned questioningly to the fourth occupant, who had listened impassively to all that had been said. "Well," he said at last, "I'm also in the Royal Air Force, but I'm a Warrant Officer. I never married, but I did father 3 children: they are all Squadron Leaders."

Air Commodore M. Barnes
Director of Public Relations (RAF), Ministry of Defence.

On a Friday evening a few years ago, a dishevelled young man was sitting in the entrance to Woking railway station begging from the homegoing commuters. In front of him was a handwritten sign which read "Falklands Veteran."

An inebriated Yuppie, returning home from a City wine bar, saw the man and immediately was overcome with alcohol-induced sympathy; he felt in his pocket for some loose change. Not finding any coins, he took out his wallet and donated a five pound note.

"Muchos gracias, Senor" said the beggar.

Squadron Leader K.R. Kendrick
Ministry of Defence

A stranger, sitting by the bar in an isolated country pub, asked the landlord for a light.

"No," said the landlord.

"But," said the stranger, a little taken aback, "I notice that you are smoking; why won't you give me a light?"

"Well," said the landlord, "If I were to give you a light, we would most probably start a conversation; you would buy me a drink, then I would buy you one in return and one thing would lead to another and, before you knew it, you would have drunk too much to be able to drive; I would then feel obliged to put you up for the night. We would end up upstairs in the flat, drinking my favourite whisky. At bedtime, you would have to sleep on the couch because we only have two bedrooms; my wife and I share one, and my 18 year old daughter has the other. Halfway through the night you would probably sneak into my daughter's bedroom, make love to her and make her pregnant. And then you would not do the decent thing and marry her."

"How can you be so sure that I would not marry her?" asked the stranger.

"Because," said the landlord, "I am not going to give you a light."

Sergeant P.T. Gallichan
RAF Church Fenton

☆ ☆ ☆

I am sure you all know of Sir Francis Drake and his naval conflict with the Spanish Armada. However, not many history books know the whole story. It all began with Sir Francis playing bowls on Plymouth Hoe when a FAX (or its Elizabethan equivalent) arrived telling of the impending trouble. Well Sir Francis, being a good staff officer and well aware of the (then) New Management Strategy for the Ministry of Defence, had not manned up all his ships; so he quickly implemented the Recall Plan (then known as the "Press Gang").

In downtown Plymouth the recruiting team were out looking for prospective sailors in the local bars when they came across a mountain of a man; 7 feet 2 inches – and that was just across the shoulders – muscles that would make Rambo look like a wimp, knuckles dragging on the ground and an IQ somewhat lower than his weight in metric tonnes; in short, good pilot material.

Anyhow, the Press Gang were in two minds about their ability to capture this prize so, walking up to the lad they asked: "What's your name?"

"TREBLE," boomed the reply.

"Fancy joining the Navy?"

"Yes, I'd love to," answered Treble.

The day before the battle Sir Francis lined up the new recruits so that he could have the pick. Seeing Treble towering above all assembled, he quickly got him on board his ship.

All was fine: the ships left on the high tide, but just a little rushed. They spotted the Armada and prepared to enter battle. However, whilst checking the equipment, it was discovered that they had forgotten the grappling irons for the boarding phase. Sir Francis, being an innovator, had the bright idea of briefing Treble to wait until they came up beside a Spanish ship and, when abeam, to put one leg over the side to hold the two ships together until they could board. So Treble waited at the side of the ship until the order came:

"OK TREBLE"

With his usual enthusiasm he stamped his leg over the side to grip the Spanish ship. However, he did it with such force that his foot went straight through the bottom of the galleon and it sank immediately.

"Hello!" thought Sir Francis, "this looks like a new tactic; I must remember to mention it to the Central Tactics and Trials Organisation on my return." Wishing to test his theory, he did exactly the same to another Spanish ship:

"OK TREBLE" – glug, glug, glug, Spanish ship Number 2.

By this time the Spanish Admiral had noticed and was getting a bit worried. Sir Francis tried it again, and the result on Ship Number 3 was the same; likewise with the fourth ship. The Spanish Admiral decided at this stage that enough was enough, and withdrew via Scotland. The English force was jubilant and signalled a triumphant post mission report back to Plymouth.

Thus the town had time to prepare a welcome appropriate to the occasion. As the fleet approached Plymouth Hoe on its triumphant return, a giant hoarding had been erected on the quay; in fact it survives to this day:

"TREBLE STAMPS ON 4 GALLEONS"

Squadron Leader J. Gilbert
RAF Spadeadam

☆ ☆ ☆

During my tour at RAF Gutersloh, Germany, in the late 1970s we enjoyed the services of a number of Army bands at our Officers' Mess dining-in nights. Towards the end of the tour, a moratorium on public spending (known at the time as The Dreaded Moriarty) threatened this pleasant arrangement. The difficulty arose because all Service units were required to make a ten percent saving on their Motor Transport (MT) running costs. Naturally the first class of journeys to be banned were things like band movements. As both an MT officer and the Officers' Mess Secretary, I was clearly going to get some searching questions from my Commanding Officer about silent guest nights.

Now it turned out that the RAF and the Army had adopted different approaches to the required ten percent savings. The Army simply restricted the amount of fuel available at their pumps to ninety percent of current consumption; the RAF monitored the mileage of each of its vehicles and controlled it to ninety percent of previous use. This meant that, if an Army vehicle brought a band to Gutersloh and refuelled (along with a jerrican or two) at an RAF pump...

For nine months, Gutersloh was the only RAF Germany station to have music at its guest nights. Inter-service co-operation of the finest kind!

Squadron Leader P. Amey
RAF Leuchars

My contribution is the story of the dyslexic pimp who bought a warehouse by mistake.

Air Marshal Sir Frank Holroyd, KBE CB MSc CEng FIEE FRAeS CBIM
Chief of Logistic Support (RAF), Ministry of Defence

The Nimrod squadron had been deployed to Sigonella for the winter. Following a long period of continuous rain, the airfield and camp area were a morass but, despite the very unpleasant conditions, the unpopular squadron commander insisted that he would still hold weekly inspections. When he reached the Supply Squadron tent he found the staff standing smartly to attention, ankle deep in mud.

"Good morning gentlemen, it's very muddy today."

"Yes Sir," replied the squadron wag "I'm standing on top of a Land Rover!"

Squadron Leader A.G. Rayment
RAF Linton-on-Ouse

A Bishop and a young lady died at the same time and went to heaven where St Peter met them at the gate. St Peter asked the young lady in and left the Bishop waiting. When St Peter came back the Bishop complained bitterly that he should have been asked in at the same time; given his calling, he suggested, there might even be a case for him to have been invited in first.

"Ah," said St Peter, "what you don't know is that she used to drive a Porsche; she put the fear of God into far more people than you ever did!"

Group Captain R.K. Hepburn

In the days when the "V-force" – Vulcan, Victor and Valiant bombers – maintained the nation's primary nuclear deterrent, the crews on Quick Reaction Alert (QRA) were never allocated a specific target until after they had been scrambled. Details were kept in a sealed envelope which was to be opened (possibly as depicted dramatically in the classic Hollywood film "Failsafe") en route to the target and after the authorities had confirmed that this was no false alarm.

Who but the RAF would supply envelopes for this Armageddon mission which were overprinted with detailed instructions for how the envelope could be re-used in the interests of economy?"

Squadron Leader J.D. Tyler
RAF Leuchars

☆ ☆ ☆

A man was out walking with his young son when they came across two dogs, and the father was mightily embarrassed when his lad demanded to know what the two dogs were doing. The best that the father's frantic thought processes could come up with was the old chestnut that the dog at the back must have sore paws and the dog in front was helping him home.

However, the father had failed to recognise that his son was a child of his times:

"Well, that's life isn't it Dad; go out of your way to help someone and you'll get screwed every time!"

Wing Commander J.O. Bates
Ministry of Defence

☆ ☆ ☆

The scene is a dusty township in the Western states of America. The State Marshal rides into town and hails a scruffy cowboy on the sidewalk:

Marshall: "Hi y'all; I'm Marshal Jones – have you seen the outlaw Kid Bean in town? He's a real bad, real mean hombre."

Cowboy: "No Marshal; but how would I recognise him if I did see him?"

Marshal: "He wearyuhs a hat made out of brown paper; a shirt and trousers made out of brown paper; his poncho is made out of brown paper. Hell, even his gunbelt and boots is made of brown paper. He's one heck of a nasty dude."

Cowboy: "Say Marshal – if he's so nasty, what is he wanted fur?"

Marshal: "Rustling."

Wing Commander R J Woodroffe
RAF Leuchars

The Annual Formal Inspection by the Air Officer Commanding (AOC) is a very traumatic occasion for most RAF stations. The great man arrives from his remote headquarters with considerable panoply, often to be met by a Guard of Honour and formal parade, and inspects every section and function of the station concerned. Station commanders, rightly or wrongly, believe that their entire future career can be affected by the impression gained of their stations on these occasions. Quite often the AOC's wife also visits and is escorted through a separate programme – not quite so formal, but equally one of those things that the station wants to run smoothly.

I remember one such occasion when the AOC was planned to arrive by air and his wife by road. Our Officer Commanding General Duties Flight – the all purpose junior officer dogsbody -was one Flying Officer Bob Constance-Tailor, affectionately known as Constant Failure; he was detailed off to meet the AOC's wife at the main gate and lead her in an escort vehicle to the Staion Commander's residence.

As the advertised time approached, Bob left his office and walked to the main gate. His escort vehicle had not yet arrived; no matter, there was still 15 minutes to go. With 5 minutes to go there was still no car and Bob, now starting to panic, telephoned the Motor Transport office.

"But it was sent 10 minutes ago" spluttered the flustered airwoman at the other end.

"Well, it's not here; get me another vehicle. NOW!" boomed Bob.

"But the vehicles are all out, and there's no drivers" she wailed.

"I don't care; get me ANYTHING, and get it NOW."

As Bob slammed the telephone down, his mind was racing, searching for excuses for the inevitable interview with the Station Commander.

The last minutes ticked by and the AOC's wife's car hove into sight precisely on time. At the same time there appeared from the other direction a mechanical runway sweeper, driven by a red faced and very flustered airwoman. Bob snapped off a crisp salute – if nothing else he had a fine military bearing – welcomed the AOC's wife and invited her to follow his vehicle.

With a roaring of engines and in a cloud of dust, the mechanical sweeper pulled away. We will never know what the AOC's wife thought of the antics of our modern day Walter Raleigh; but she could not but be impressed by how spotlessly clean we kept our roads!

Group Captain P.J. Scott
Ministry of Defence

☆ ☆ ☆

I was once on a joint-service course held in London. We were a mixed bunch of junior officers from varied backgrounds and were being hosted by a famous Army regiment who shall remain nameless. On the first morning of the course we all gathered in the dining room for breakfast in our different working dress. I could not help noticing that one Army officer was wearing his pith helmet and was particularly subdued. My colleague, another Flight Lieutenant, asked the hatted gentleman to pass the salt. A simple enough request, one would think; however he was met by the most disgusted glare, closely followed by the officer and his helmet stomping out of the Mess. "Strange", thought my friend, who then helped himself to the salt and finished his food in silence.

We had all forgotten the incident when, next morning, we were gathered again for breakfast; this time there was a different chap wearing his pith helmet. Probably because he did not want to reach over the table, my friend asked this officer to pass the butter for his toast. The table erupted and, giving the filthiest look I have ever seen, the helmeted one again stormed out.

Obviously to avoid further embarrassment my friend was taken aside; it was explained to him that one of the oldest traditions of that particular regiment was that, if an officer wore his hat at breakfast then, under pain of death, no-one but no-one must speak to him.

My friend was not to be outdone. The next day he arrived at the breakfast table wearing the muddiest pair of boots imaginable. He proceeded to sit at a table where he was literally surrounded by pith-hatted Guards (Oops!) officers. When his food arrived, he took off his boots and plonked them firmly on the plate of the gentleman opposite. After the expected commotion had died down, he sounded surprised and slowly and carefully explained to the angry crowd that it was simply one of the oldest traditions of the Royal Air Force; that is, if an officer places his boots in your breakfast, he only wants you to pass the salt!

Flight Lieutenant D.P. Lord
RAF Valley

☆ ☆ ☆

Two Germans, visiting the UK for the first time, arrived in Dover; whilst waiting for the ferry to dock, they discussed what they wanted to do first. They decided that they wanted to try some English beer, but did not know any brand names to ask for.

"Never mind," said one, "we will look at the advertising hoardings for a name."

Arriving in the town, they saw a large hoarding with a poster saying:

Drink Eno's – it makes you feel younger.

They entered a quality hotel, went to the bar and ordered two pints of Eno's. The barman, used to odd requests from foreigners, served two pints of Eno's liversalts. After their fifth pint, the first German turned to the second and said:

"Has it made you feel any younger?"

"I think so," said the second "because I have just done something extremely childish."

Squadron Leader M.D. Green
RAF Brawdy

☆ ☆ ☆

After dinner speeches, like good short stories, should always be brief. It is said that Somerset Maugham visiting a well-known girls' public school offered a prize for the best short story. The essential ingredients, he advised, were religion, royalty, sex and mystery. The prize had to go to the girl who wrote:

"Christ", said the Princess, I'm pregnant. Who done it?"

Air Marshal Sir David Parry-Evans, KCB CBE
Air Member for Personnel, Ministry of Defence

☆ ☆ ☆

The proud owner of a brand new Beech King Air arrived early at his local aerodrome to await the aircraft's arrival on a delivery flight from the USA. Weather conditions were ideal, with a brisk south easterly wind causing the airfield to be operating on the short Runway 11, with larger aircraft using the longer Runway 21.

On time, Air Traffic Control telephoned to say that the aircraft was inbound, and the owner and some friends gathered outside the clubhouse to watch its arrival.

Expecting the aircraft to land on Runway 21, their excitement turned to surprise when they saw it, despite the tailwind, apparently making an approach to Runway 03 – the other end of Runway 21. To their relief, at the last moment the aircraft overshot and went into a gentle orbit of the airfield. A friend tried to reassure the owner, explaining that the pilot was probably now repositioning for an approach to the correct runway. However, their relief was short-lived as they suddenly realised that the orbit had been used to position the aircraft for an approach to Runway 29 - the other end of Runway 11; downwind again, but now on a short runway!

This time there was no overshoot. The aircraft bounced first halfway down the runway; then bounced again threequarters of the way down, finally leaving the runway behind; it exited the airfield through the boundary fence, crossed the main dual carriageway running alongside the airfield – passing between the lamp posts as it went – and finally came to rest in a layby on the far side.

Emergency services, the owner and his friends raced to the scene. The aircraft was a write-off although the pilot had managed to extricate himself from the wreckage with only cuts and bruises.

"What on earth were you doing?" exclaimed the owner, now entering a state of shock.

"I'm terribly sorry," replied the pilot, "I couldn't stop – the brakes didn't work."

"That really isn't surprising," retorted the owner, "the wheels need to be in contact with the ground to achieve the best effect; you were still airborne when you went through the fence!"

Squadron Leader I.M. Sheeley
RAF Leuchars

☆ ☆ ☆

"Dad," said the baby polar bear, "are you a real polar bear?"

"Yes" said his father.

"Is Mummy a real polar bear?" said the baby.

"Yes, of course" said his father.

"Are you absolutely sure that both you and Mummy are real polar bears?" persisted the young bear.

"Of course we are," said the father crossly, "what on earth is the matter?"

"Well, why am I so bloody cold?"

Group Captain B.A. Wright
Ministry of Defence

☆ ☆ ☆

A Commander-in-Chief was playing a round of golf with one of his subordinates, and was playing atrociously. Being a Commander-in-Chief, he had a ready stock of excuses; a dog had distracted him, a gust of wind had caught him, the players in front were in the way. His career-conscious and very tactful subordinate accepted all of these; he even offered some new ones of his own.

By the time they reached the fourteenth tee, both had run out of excuses and the subordinate had run out of tact. After yet another appallingly short drive from this tee the Commander-in-Chief said:

"You know, I think I have identified my problem; I'm standing too close to the ball as I drive."

"Yes Sir," said the subordinate, "and immediately afterwards!"

Group Captain J.K. Walters
Commanding Officer, RAF Church Fenton

The Martians sent a fact finding mission to Earth some years ago. Their flying saucer collected 3 human beings as specimens for study. On return to Mars, each man was placed in isolation in the Martian desert, given 2 solid stainless steel spherical balls, and watched to see how he would react.

After 3 weeks, the Martian scientist reported the results to his Director:

"Director" he said, "the first man was taken from the area known as Asia; he is Chinese and is a train driver."

"How has he done?" asked the Director.

"Well Sir, in 3 weeks he has learned how to juggle the 2 balls; he can now keep them in the air for up to 16 minutes at a time."

"Reasonable," said the Director, "and how about the second man?"

"Number 2 is from an area called Africa; he is a farmer from a country known as Kenya. Over the last 3 weeks he has learned how to spin one ball clockwise on top of his index finger, with the other one balanced on top and spinning in an anticlockwise direction. He can keep this going for up to 27 minutes."

Contra-rotating balls!" exclaimed the Director, "most encouraging. What about the last human?"

"Well, he is from Europe, from a country called Britain. He is a military man from the air section of their military forces – a Supply Officer in what is known as The Royal Air Force."

"And what has he achieved, then?" asked the Director.

"Well Sir, I am afraid that he has lost one and broken the other!"

Group Captain R. Dixon
Ministry of Defence, Harrogate

☆ ☆ ☆

An Englishman, a Frenchman and a Russian were sitting around a table at a cafe in Paris; having exhausted such weighty topics as the recent events in Europe and CFE, the conversation drifted to what constitutes true happiness.

"Well," said the Englishman, "my definition of true happiness is when, after a hard day at the office, you return home late to your loving wife; she greets you at the door with a kiss, takes your coat, brings a gin and tonic to the table by your favourite armchair, fetches your slippers and tells you that your favourite dinner will be ready in 20 minutes."

"Ah," said the Frenchman, "you English have no romance; no romance in your hearts whatsoever. True happiness is when you kiss your wife goodbye before catching your plane for the afternoon meeting in Nice. The meeting is concluded very satisfactorily, and much earlier than expected, so you take your business associate – who happens to be a very attractive young lady – to the local bistro where, over coffee, you find that you have many interests in common. You invite her to join you later at the best restaurant in town and she accepts. So you have the candlelight dinner, an excellent meal with maybe just a little bit too much excellent wine. You escort this lovely young lady back to her hotel and, with one thing leading to another, you wake up in her arms the following morning. Eventually you part, but with no regrets on either side. That, my friends, is true happiness."

"You are both wrong," said the Russian, "true happiness is when you have had a hard day at the office; you return home to your small apartment at the top of the block of flats; you eat your meal – which you have to cook yourself – off the last of your uncracked plates, wash it down with a couple of stiff vodkas of doubtful quality, and retire to bed early because the heating has failed and there is nothing else to do. You are in this deep sleep when suddenly you are woken by this terrible banging on the door; you ignore it for some little time, but the banging gets louder and eventually a voice shouts: "This is the KGB, open up or we will break the door down." Shaking with trepidation you open up; three KGB gorillas burst in, grab you and say: Ivan Ivanovitch, you are a traitor, you are under arrest, come with us." True happiness, my friends, is when you are then able to say "But I am not Ivan Ivanovitch; he lives next door."'"

Group Captain C.J. Sturt
Headquarters Strike Command

☆ ☆ ☆

At a scientific convention in Moscow, a Russian delegate leaned across to his American counterpart and asked if it was true that the Americans had taken to using lawyers instead of rats for scientific experiments.

"It sure is," said the American, "particularly in my home state of California. The rationale is firstly that there are more lawyers than rats in California and secondly that there is less likelihood of the scientists becoming emotionally involved with the subjects."

Wing Commander J.A. Upham
RAF Henlow

☆ ☆ ☆

A student navigator from the Air Navigation School at RAF Finningley made an appointment to see the Medical Officer. When his appointment was called he marched into the Medical Officer's office, came smartly to attention and snapped off a smart salute.

"Sit down and relax," said the doctor, "what seems to be the problem?"

The student sat down and removed his uniform hat to reveal a frog actually growing out of the top of his head.

"Good Lord!" said the Medical Officer; "how on earth did that happen?"

"I dunno," said the frog; "it started off as a wart on my bum!"

Squadron Leader D.A.R. Hinchliffe
RAF Church Fenton

☆ ☆ ☆

Most people are familiar with the better known Christmas traditions, but I have encountered very few who know the origin of the little doll on the top of the Christmas tree.

Once upon a time, Father Christmas had a little girl helper. One Christmas Eve, exhausted by all the preparations for the big delivery run that night, he asked her to deal with any visitors while he took a short nap in front of the log fire before setting off on his run. He was just dozing off when she tapped at the door and entered.

"Father Christmas," she said, "there is a man at the door with some more presents."

"Get him to put them on the sleigh," he replied irritably, "and leave me in peace."

He settled back in his armchair but, within five minutes, she was back.

"Father Christmas; some more reindeer food has arrived."

"Give it to the deer, then; and LEAVE ME ALONE," he shouted.

Unbelievably, just as his eyelids closed for the third time, she entered again.

"Father Christmas," she said sweetly, "there's a man outside with another Christmas tree; where shall I put it?"

Squadron Leader (Retired) M.J. Fletcher
RAF Linton on Ouse

☆ ☆ ☆

After years of scrimping and saving, a Russian peasant decided that he could now afford a car. He went to the local LADA agent, ordered one and paid the deposit.

"You realise, of course, that there is a long waiting list for these cars," said the salesman, "yours will be delivered in ten years time."

"Morning or afternoon?" asked the customer.

"No idea," said the salesman, "why?"

"It's just that the gas man is coming in the morning."

Wing Commander J.A. Upham
RAF Henlow

☆ ☆ ☆

In the mid 1980s, when relationships between the UK and China started to thaw, the RAF hosted a visiting party of senior officers from the Air Force of the People's Republic of China. At the end of the visit, which had lasted several days, the Chinese delegation invited a large RAF contingent to a farewell cocktail party at the official residence of the Chinese

Air Attache in London. As is usual on these occasions, protocol demanded that the guest list should include many senior RAF officers who had had little to do with the visit, and who knew very little of its purpose.

One of this number, an Air Vice Marshal, found himself in a group which included the Chinese Ambassador. Desperately casting around for a topic of conversation, the Air Vice Marshal announced that he was a great lover of Chinese food.

"Oh really," said the Ambassador, "and what is your favourite dish?"

The Air Vice Marshal thought for a moment, and then replied "Number 34".

Anon

☆ ☆ ☆

While surprised to find himself dead, the Pope was pleased to have arrived at the Pearly Gates with so little difficulty. Unfortunately, they appeared firmly padlocked, but there was a small notice which read:

"CLOSED FOR PUBLIC HOLIDAY – USE SIDE ENTRANCE"

He floated round to a small wicker gate at the side of the main entrance to Heaven, and was greeted somewhat perfunctorily by a rather scruffy cherubim, who appeared to have drawn the short straw for gate duty on this holiday.

"Welcome to Heaven." recited the cherubim. "Your room has your name on it. If you drop your bags there now, you may just catch the big parade."

Increasingly irritated by his treatment, the Pope found his room, dropped his bag, and followed the sound of celestial brass bands to find the parade. Suddenly as he came out into the open, he could see the infinite multitude stretching into the distance; in the foreground was the majestic parade with God himself at the head, and at his right hand a proud figure decked in light blue with a broad gold halo over his head. This was not how the Pope had imagined Heaven, and he retired to his room to a restless night's sleep.

The next morning there was a knock at the door; it was St Peter:

"Sorry I wasn't there to meet you when you arrived but, as you probably gathered, we were all at the big celebration parade. I hope that all the arrangements were satisfactory."

"I wouldn't wish to complain," said the Pope in a somewhat stiff Polish-Italian accent, "but I was a little surprised that when God's representative on Earth ascends to Heaven, everyone is out at a great military parade for some man in light blue with a single broad gold halo."

"You must look at it from our point of view," said St Peter, "you are the 35th Pope we have had, but that was the first time we had ever seen an Air Commodore"

Air Commodore T. Garden
Ministry of Defence

☆ ☆ ☆

A young man, the sole survivor of a plane crash, had been marooned on a desert island for ten years. One morning a large motor cruiser appeared on the horizon and anchored in his lagoon. Its sole occupant, a very attractive young lady, jumped over the side wearing scuba gear and disappeared into the depths. By the time the young man had made his way to the shore, she had emerged from the lagoon and was lying on the beach in the sun. He joined her.

"How amazing!" she gasped when he had explained his presence, "but you are in luck. I have come over from a civilised and inhabited island only one hundred miles away, and I will gladly take you back tonight."

"Thank you," he whispered, unable to believe his luck.

"I really can't understand," continued the girl "how you have managed to survive for so long on this island. There is only one palm tree, no other significant vegetation, and there appear to be no animals."

"You're right," said the young man, "I have led an amazingly frugal existence. I get the odd coconut from the tree. I tried to find something to use as a fishing spear, but without success; however I did make a net out of the fibres of my shirt, so I catch quite a few fish, which I eat raw; I also dig for clams."

"Well, it certainly seems to have done you no harm," breathed the girl, gazing admiringly at his athletic physique and fluttering her eyelashes. "Tell me, do you drink?"

"I did," said the man "but obviously I haven't had any for ten years."

Slowly and voluptuously the girl slid open a zip pocket on the right breast of her wetsuit, took out a flask of whisky, and handed it to him.

"Gosh, that was good," he said, handing it back.

"Do you smoke?" asked the girl, snuggling closer to him.

"Yes," he replied, "although, as I haven't had one for ten years, I was thinking of giving it up – tomorrow."

She moved closer still and unzipped another pocket in her left breast. Taking out a packet of cigarettes and some matches, she lit two cigarettes and passed one to him.

"What bliss," he sighed, drawing on the cigarette and taking another swig of whisky.

The girl reached up to the centre zip of her wetsuit and started drawing it slowly down her front.

"Tell me," she breathed throatily, "would you like to play around?"

"Good Lord," he exclaimed "have you got a set of golf clubs in there?"

"No, silly," she laughed, "I was talking about having a bit of fun, if you know what I mean."

"Ah," he said "I do know what you mean; but I was rather young when we crashed and actually I am still a virgin."

"Perhaps we should do something about that, too," whispered the girl, drawing him towards her...

"How was that then?" said the girl fifteen minutes later.

"Unbelievable," sighed the young man, "but look what it's done to my clam digger!"

Group Captain J.K. Walters
Commanding Officer, RAF Church Fenton

☆ ☆ ☆

An Admiral, a General and an Air Marshal arrived in Heaven on the same day after an unfortunate train accident on the way to the Ministry of Defence. As they entered the Pearly Gates, St Peter issued each officer with a halo and explained to them that, whilst Heaven was in general an easy going place, lewd thoughts were not allowed and that it would be immediately obvious to the staff if residents allowed their minds to wander in this direction. Punishment for such transgressions would be swift and severe.

After some weeks of pure thought, the three officers were taking a stroll when they spied a gorgeous nymph coming in their direction. The Air Marshal was particularly taken with the lady but, as his mind began to wander, there was a loud crash and his halo fell off. The General, seeing St Peter approaching in a seething rage, quickly bent down to recover his friend's halo. Immediately, there was a second resounding crash as the Admiral's halo fell off.

Squadron Leader C.W. Ness
Headquarters Strike Command

The arrival of the NATO Tactical Evaluation Team (TAC-EVAL) is always a traumatic occasion on a front-line RAF station. The multi-national team, controlled by a faceless multi-national headquarters is wont to descend on a station, totally unannounced, and start a simulated no-notice war. They have the ability to simulate, or actually produce, every kind of problem that could possibly be imagined – air attacks, fires, intruders on the ground, and every conceivable kind of damage and unserviceability. At the end of this process, which can last up to a week, woe betide any station which has not coped with everything that the team can throw at it. Needless to say, there is always a certain element of inter-nation rivalry; and not always as friendly as one might imagine.

The scenario for this particular story is Day 4 of a TAC-EVAL on an RAF Germany Buccaneer base in the mid 1970s. An RAF sergeant armourer and his team of 3 airmen have been tasked with loading bombs on to an aircraft in a Hardened Aircraft Shelter. Thanks to the other antics of the TACEVAL team, the RAF team are tired, cold and extremely hungry. In walks one of the evaluation team, a Dutch major.

Dutch Major: "What would you do if you came under attack from 5 intruders?"

RAF Sergeant: "Only 5 Sir – easy. Half of my team would rush outside to fight off the intruders while the other half carried on loading the weapons."

Dutch Major: "OK. But what if there were 10 intruders?"

RAF Sergeant: "That would be a little more difficult, Sir. I would collect my team around me; we would rush outside, fight off the intruders, and then return to complete the weapon loading."

Dutch Major: "And if there were 100 intruders?"

RAF Sergeant: "I think you already know the answer to that one, Sir. I would collect my team around me; we would rush outside. And then we would run like Hell – like your lot did in 1939!"

Wing Commander M. Davies, MSc BSc CEng MIMechE
RAF Coningsby

An Englishman, an Irishman and a Scotsman went to watch the Olympic Games. They had no tickets but turned up at the stadium hoping for inspiration on how to effect entry. The Englishman looked around and spotted a clothes prop holding up a line of washing in a garden; this gave him an idea.

Watched by his two colleagues he took the prop, walked up to the steward on the competitors' gate and said crisply: "Smith, England, Pole Vault." The Scotsman was impressed and, cottoning on quickly, went to a nearby backyard and removed the lid from a small dustbin. He marched up to the steward, recited "McTavish, Scotland, Discus," and was waved through.

The Irishman was amazed at the ease with which this trick had worked and, not to be outdone, walked on to an adjacent building site and picked up a roll of barbed wire. Jauntily approaching the steward, he sang out confidently: "Murphy, Ireland, Fencing."

Wing Commander S.D. McCullouch
Ministry of Defence

☆ ☆ ☆

A Group Captain, recently retired from the Administrative (Secretarial) Branch was to be found, six months later, bored to the point of frustration. The garden was in bloom, the windows painted, house decorated; and no-one seemed to want his services as a consultant. "I'm still in my prime!"

he shouted to nobody in particular (his wife was at the Bridge Club).

Flicking through the local newspaper, an advertisement caught his eye: "Wanted: person with initiative, willing to make decisions, to assist in farm management. Telephone XXXX for interview." He called the number, and was invited to report to a nearby farm for an interview the following morning.

He arrived at the farm promptly at 9am, wearing his best suit. Farmer Jessop seemed impressed with the Group Captain's background and, having fixed him up with some old clothes, led him round to the back of the barn. He showed him a large pile of steaming manure and invited him to spread it over the adjacent field as a test of his suitability for the job. The Group Captain had always kept himself fairly fit; he set to work with a will and, by 11am had called the farmer to say that the job was finished.

The farmer seemed quite impressed:

"One more test," he said, "and the job is yours."

He led the Group Captain to another field, pointed out an enormous pile of potatoes and gave him a large board with three different sized holes cut in it. For this test, the potatoes had to be sorted into three piles reflecting the different hole sizes. The farmer went away.

At 5pm, having heard nothing, the farmer returned. The Group Captain was sitting on a bucket, weeping; the pile of potatoes appeared untouched.

"Don't be upset, lad," said the farmer. "Nowt has changed sin' I were in t'trenches. Officers can always spread s★★t, but ask them to make a decision... You stick to what 'ee does best."

Squadron Leader A.E. Powell
Ministry of Defence

☆ ☆ ☆

Three sales representatives working for the same firm were tired of always taking clients out to lunch. They decided that one day they would meet at a particular country pub for a quiet lunch, well out of sight of the Sales Director.

The appointed date and time arrived and they met in the pub car park at noon, as arranged. The only other car in the car park was a Rolls-Royce, gleaming splendidly in the sunshine. They entered the saloon bar to find only one other customer there. He was dressed in a flat hat, a waistcoat, corduroy trousers with string round the knees, and old wellies. They bade him good day and asked him if he knew who owned the Rolls. He replied that the car was his.

As the conversation rambled on one of the reps said to the owner of the Rolls-Royce:

"I hope you don't mind my saying this but you seem a fairly ordinary sort of bloke; and yet you own and run a Rolls-Royce. What job do you do?"

Oh, I'm the council rat catcher," replied the man.

"Gosh," said the salesman, "you must have an enormous salary."

"No," replied the workman, "the wages are pretty poor, but I make the money on the extras."

"What do you mean?" asked the rep.

"Well," said the rat catcher, "I catch 1500 rats per week and get a bounty of 5p per rat from the County Council. I skin and debone the rats and get 6p per pound for the meat; it goes to a catfood factory. I cure the skins and sell them for 10p each to a firm making moleskin trousers. I sell the bones to the glue factory for 3p per pound. Also, I collect all the whiskers and sell them to a paintbrush manufacturer at 45p per bushel. Now, let me see; have I covered everything? Ah, no, there are the droppings.

"What on earth do you do with the droppings?" asked the salesman.

"Well," said the rat catcher, "I dry them and sell them for 2p per pound to a factory in Birmingham which makes screwdriver handles."

"What do the firm do with the droppings?" asked the puzzled rep. "You can't make screwdriver handles out of them.

"Of course you can," replied the man, "haven't you ever heard of ratchet handled screwdrivers?"

Wing Commander J.S.R. Mays
Ministry of Defence

☆ ☆ ☆

A fabulously rich Arab sheik lay on his deathbed, his family gathered around him; all were weeping silently as it became obvious that the great man's final moments were approaching.

"Achmed," he croaked, "you are my firstborn, my eldest son; the future of the tribe lies in your hands. I should like to leave you something to remember me by. I know that you have always been interested in boats, so I have instructed the Chancellor to buy you the QEII as a private yacht."

"Thank you, my father," wept Achmed.

"Mohanad, my big second son," continued the sheik in a quavering voice, "I also have thought of something for you. I know that you have always been interested in aeroplanes – model ones originally, but more recently the real thing; you have gained your pilot's licence, and your instructors think you have great potential. I have instructed the Chancellor to buy you a Concorde as an executive jet."

"I am overwhelmed, my father," said the second son.

"Feizal, my youngest son," continued the sheik, "you are only twelve years old. You are the apple of my eye, but I know very little about your interests or desires. Tell me what I can give you to remember me by."

"Oh my beloved father," piped the youngest, "I was unprepared for the question; but there is one thing that I have always wanted: a cowboy outfit."

"It shall be done," croaked the sheik and, turning to his Chancellor, he said: "I want you to leave for London, immediately. You are to make arrangements to buy the Army Air Corps."

Wing Commander J.M.A. Mayo
RAF Stafford

☆ ☆ ☆

A misfortune befell a RAF aircraft flying in the Far East and the crew, a pilot and a navigator, baled out and parachuted into the jungle. They had been unable to transmit a distress message and, because of the thick jungle canopy, the wreckage of the aircraft could not have been seen from the air. They decided that they would have to walk out.

After three days they were thoroughly demoralised, dirty, sweaty, covered in leeches, and very tired. Just then they came to a clearing with a beautiful, crystal clear pond and a cool waterfall. To them, in their state, this was paradise. They stripped off and jumped into the water. The navigator swam out to the centre of the pool and lay on his back enjoying a good soak. The pilot, a bit of a wimp, stayed near the shore, washing himself.

Suddenly, the navigator heard a rustling in the jungle and an enormous priapic male ape appeared. The pilot, having his back to the beast, did not see it and the navigator, dumbstruck by the sight, was unable to warn the pilot of its approach. It ran down to the water's edge, grabbed the pilot and ran off into the jungle. The screams from the pilot were terrible – a sound never to be forgotten by the navigator as he was forced to continue his survival journey solo.

About a month later, the navigator was back at base, standing in the bar having his usual pre-dinner gin and tonic, when the pilot walked in. The navigator was very embarrassed, especially about his failure to warn the pilot of the priapic ape's approach. But he was relieved to see that his colleague appeared well – indeed, he looked very fit with a sparkle in his eyes.

"I'm glad to see you made it back," said the navigator, striding over to the pilot, "and I'm happy you are not hurt."

"Hurt, hurt, hurt," screamed the pilot, the sparkle in his eyes turning to fire, "do you know, he hasn't written, he hasn't telephoned..."

Squadron Leader J. Gilbert
RAF Spadeadam

☆ ☆ ☆

Certain ex-members of a revered and famous air defence squadron are prone to meeting periodically in London and having a very good time. After one such evening, some years ago, two of them had become separated from the rest and they were ... well ... lost.

After some moderately incoherent enquiries of those few locals still on the streets at this late hour, they discovered that they were in Lambeth and that a No 92 Bus would take them to their hotel. After standing vainly at the appropriate bus-stop for at least an hour, our friends realised that the last bus had probably gone. However, they noticed a London Transport garage just down the road and decided to use their initiative and "borrow" a bus.

In a fit of enthusiasm, one of our heroes said that he would stand guard in the street "just in case anyone too sensible was to come along" whilst the second went into the garage to "liberate" a bus.

Standing outside, cold, lonely and somewhat apprehensive, our first hero could hear an engine being started, revving up and dying away again... and again... and again; but at last out of the garage came a big, red, double decked, 58 seater London omnibus.

"All aboard," cried his friend from the driver's seat.

"What on earth took you so long?" snapped the exasperated first hero.

"Patience now," replied the other, "I had to move a lot of buses out of the way; No 92 was parked right at the back!"

Squadron Leader J.M. Henson
Ministry of Defence

A blind parachutist, when asked how on earth he managed to do it replied:

UPSIDE DOWN . . .

"Quite easily; I am told how and when to jump, my hand is placed on the parachute release ring and out I go. I count one thousand, two thousand, three thousand, then pull the ripcord and descend to earth."

"But how do you know when you are nearing the ground?"

"Well, I have developed a very keen sense of smell, and I can smell trees and grass from approximately 300 feet."

"Yes, but how do you know when to lift your feet for the final landing?"

"Oh. When the dog's lead goes slack!"

Flight Lieutenant I.T. Lucas
RAF Stafford

☆ ☆ ☆

An elderly and worldly wise senior officer was discussing the question of sex with his young athletic aide. The senior officer considered sex to be vastly overrated, suggesting that it was mostly hard work and very little pleasure; he would prefer a round of golf any time. His aide disagreed most strongly; he considered that there was very little work involved in sex, only pleasure. He could think of nothing more pleasurable to do whenever the opportunity presented itself.

It was clear that the two officers were so far apart in their views on the matter that they would never reach agreement. They therefore decided to get another opinion from the Personal Assistant, a sergeant. The senior officer explained to this worthy that he and his aide had a fundamental disagreement over whether sex was a pleasure or was hard work.

Without hesitation the sergeant declared that sex was total pleasure. The proof, he opined, was that if there was any work involved at all then the officers would expect their NCOs to do it for them!

Group Captain W.G. Gambold
Ministry of Defence

☆ ☆ ☆

A travelling circus was on tour in Ireland when one of its bull elephants died. As they were working to a very tight schedule and did not own a JCB excavator, the problems of burying the body appeared insurmountable. In desperation the circus owner directed that the elephant's body should be placed in the back of a large high sided truck, together with two circus hands equipped with very sharp knives. The men were detailed to spend the journey to the next showground cutting the body into small pieces and throwing them individually into hedgerows and ditches as the journey progressed.

The gruesome and exhausting task occupied most of the journey but, with about five miles to go, the men were down to the last piece of elephant – a complete set of genitalia – which they hurled over the high stone wall that they were passing at the time.

As bad luck would have it the wall in question was the boundary wall of a nunnery, and the last piece of elephant landed quivering at the feet of a novice nun meditating at the foot of the garden. She rushed off to the Mother Superior, gibbering hysterically that something awful had flown over the wall. The Mother Superior accompanied her back to the bottom of the garden and looked at the mess in horror.

"Mother of God," she cried, crossing herself, "the Protestants have got Father O'Flaherty!"

Group Captain J.K. Walters
Commanding Officer, RAF Church Fenton

☆ ☆ ☆

A Station Commander returned from morning briefing and walked into his outer office looking rather down in the dumps. His Personal Assistant, an extremely attractive blonde with legs right up to her chin, noticed his demeanour.

"What's the matter, Sir?" she asked.

"Nothing for you to worry about, Sharon," came the reply, "it's just that it is my birthday and no-one seems to have remembered."

Sharon came out with an offer that might even have brought Lord Lucan out of hiding:

"Why don't you come round to my place tonight and I'll see if I can cheer you up?"

The Station Commander gulped, broke into a sweat, and sat down suddenly. Then he stood up, held his stomach in as best he could, and affected the language that he had heard the young officers of Sharon's generation use:

"Right on, babe; sounds groovy. I'll swing by about seven." He retired to his inner office, humming "Are you lonesome tonight."

At precisely 7pm Sharon's doorbell rang. She opened the door and was almost rendered unconscious by the waft of Old

Spice. A large bunch of flowers was thrust towards her; she then remembered seeing a junior officer crawling around the daffodil patch outside Station Headquarters that afternoon.

"Please come in, Sir and make yourself at home."

"Cut out the Sir bit, honey. Just call me Python; it's my nickname from the old days on my front-line squadron."

"OK Python," said Sharon, not keen to learn the derivation, "you just wait here and I'll go and slip into something more comfortable." She left the room.

Five minutes later, "Python" was getting restless; after ten minutes he could stand it no longer. Striding to the door through which Sharon had left, he pushed it open to discover: Sharon in a paper hat, his wife in a new dress and all his squadron commanders in their best suits and accompanied by their wives. It was a surprise party – particularly for him as he was, by now, wearing only his socks!

Flying Officer P.A. Martin
RAF Church Fenton

☆ ☆ ☆

A young man in a pub offered to show the landlord a tapdancing duck in exchange for a free drink. When the landlord agreed, the young man opened his haversack and extracted, in turn, a beautifully decorated biscuit tin and a duck. Sure enough, when he placed the duck on the tin it gave a performance worthy of one of the stars of Forty Second Street.

The landlord, seeing the potential of this act, bought it from the young man for a considerable sum. Later that week,

he saw the young man in the street and complained that the
duck had never performed since that night. The young man
asked if he had looked inside the tin.

"No," said the landlord, "why should I?"

"Well," replied the young man, "perhaps the candle has
gone out!"

Squadron Leader (Retired) M.J. Fletcher
RAF Linton-on-Ouse.

☆ ☆ ☆

Having concluded all pressing business at her weekly Cabinet
meeting, the Prime Minister turned to her colleagues and
said:

"Gentlemen, as well you know I am the first female
Prime Minister of this country and look like being one
of the longest serving. Of late my thoughts have turned to
where I should be buried when I die. I should like you all to
give thought to a suitable location – your suggestions, please,
at next Thursday's meeting."

The following Thursday duly arrived but no-one save
the Chancellor of the Exchequer had come up with any
ideas.

"Prime Minister," said the Chancellor, "I have given your
remit a great deal of thought and have reached the conclusion
that you should be buried in Jerusalem."

"Jerusalem!" exclaimed the Prime Minister, "why ever
there?"

"Just consider it Ma'am," replied the Chancellor, "the
Middle East is the hotbed of world politics. Every time that

part of the world is mentioned in the media, people will instantly conjure up a picture of Jerusalem and remember that you are buried there. Better yet," he continued, seeing that his argument was beginning to sway the lady, "I have been able to secure a burial plot in the Garden of Gethsemane."

The Prime Minister, now completely won over, was positively glowing about the idea.

"There is, however, just one minor snag, Prime Minister; I have had to pay £100,000 for the plot."

"What!" she exclaimed, "£100,000 for three days?"

Master Air Loadmaster P. Milburn
RAF Brize Norton

☆ ☆ ☆

Three NATO Army officers were dining together after an international meeting at Supreme Headquarters Allied Powers Europe – SHAPE. As the brandy flowed, the conversation turned to their love lives.

"When I leave home in the mornings," said the German major, "I always give my wife the most passionate kiss on the doorstep. It takes me half an hour to get to work and then another half an hour to wash off all the lipstick. Now that, gentlemen, is not a measure of the quality of her lipstick; it is a measure of the depths of her passion."

The British major, quick as a flash, retorted:

"When I leave home, I kiss my wife on her hand. She misses me so much that it is still warm when I return. Now that, gentlemen, is not a measure of her blood circulation, but of how much she loves and adores me."

UPSIDE DOWN . . .

The Belgian major, who had been listening intently, could not be outdone:

"Gentlemen," he said, "When I leave home in the morning, I give my wife a smack on her bottom. When I get back, it is still quivering. Now that, gentlemen, is not a reflection on the properties of my wife's bottom; it is a measure of the length of my working day!"

Group Captain N.M. Griffiths
Commanding Officer, RAF Stafford

☆ ☆ ☆

An airman who was carpeted for being late for work offered the following explanation:

"I was walking to the camp at my usual time, when I decided to have a smoke. As I was facing into the wind, I turned round in order to light the cigarette. After I had lit it I carried on walking and it was only when I arrived back at the door of my Married Quarter that I realised my error."

Warrant Officer P.M.C. Holland
RAF Brize Norton

☆ ☆ ☆

A young Police Constable on the beat took a pair of boots into the local cobblers for repair. Unfortunately he misplaced the ticket and, before he could do anything about it, he was promoted to Sergeant and posted to another division. As a result, the boots completely slipped his mind.

Over the years his career progressed and, some twenty years later, on promotion to Chief Inspector, he found himself posted back to the same station where he had started life as a young PC.

As luck would have it, when he was moving into his new office, he dropped an old notebook and out fell the ticket for his old boots.

Out of curiosity he took the ticket and went in search of the old cobblers shop. He found it without difficulty, handed in the ticket and asked if the boots were still there.

"You must be joking," said the assistant, "this shop has changed hands four times in the last twenty years. Still, I'll go and ask in the workshop."

After about ten minutes the assistant emerged from the back of the shop and announced:

"They should be ready on Friday."

Wing Commander I. Sloss
RAF Swanton Morley

Somewhere in Eastern Europe in the early years of this century, a peasant was digging in the fields when he came across an antique but clearly very valuable ring. In an attempt to clean it, he rubbed it on his threadbare shirt. With a flash of light a genie appeared, anxious to grant the peasant three wishes.

"I wish," said the Peasant, "that I could escape the poverty and drudgery of this existence and live in a beautiful castle with servants to look after my every need."

"Fine," said the genie, "anything else?"

"Well, I should also like to be a prince with a beautiful golden haired princess to share life with me."

"Right," said the genie, "no problem; what about the last wish?"

"Perhaps most of all," said the peasant, "I should like to make my mark in the history of our great nation."

Suddenly there was a great flash of light and the peasant found himself being gently shaken awake. As he emerged from his slumbers he found himself in a beautiful four-poster bed with silken covers. He could see that his bedchamber was in a fine castle with the trappings of wealth and luxury all around him. Out of the window he could see his kingdom stretching into the distance. Lush green fields, abundant with crops, were illuminated by the soft morning sunlight. The birds were singing and a gentle breeze was playing through the trees.

He turned his attention to whoever was shaking him, to realize that it was a beautiful princess with long golden hair and eyes of the deepest blue which portrayed a look of deep affection. As he gradually emerged further from his slumbers he began to recognise her words as:

"Wake up Franz Ferdinand; it's time to leave for Sarajevo."

Air Chief Marshal Sir Patrick Hine, GCB ADC FRAeS CBIM
Air Officer Commanding-in-Chief Strike Command

☆ ☆ ☆

EXTRACT FROM THE SIGNAL LOG OF THE MESSAGE CENTRE, MALAYAN COUNTY SECTION, FORCE 136 HEADQUARTERS, KANDY

From Commander in Field:

WILL YOU HALF WITTED BASTARDS FOR CHRISSAKE OUTFINGER SOONEST STOP FIRST YOU SEND ME SIZE SIX BOOTS STOP THEN YOU SEND ME NO BOOTS STOP THEN YOU SEND ME TWO LEFT REPEAT TWO LEFT BLOODY BOOTS STOP IT IS HIGH TIME YOU GOT YOUR HEADS OUT OF YOUR BACKSIDES STOP DO YOU WANT ME TO CONTINUE THIS BLOODY WAR OR NOT QUERY

From HQ:

AYE WILL NOT REPEAT NOT TOLERATE THE USE OF INTEMPERATE AND IMPROPER LANGUAGE FROM OFFICERS IN THE FIELD STOP REASONS ARE TWOFOLD STOP ONE IT IS UNMILITARY AND UNGEN-TLEMANLY STOP TWO THE CYPHER CLERKS ARE VOLUNTEER LADIES STOP THIS SORT OF BEHAVIOUR WILL GET YOU NOWHERE STOP

From Commander in Field:

NOR WILL TWO LEFT BLOODY BOOTS STOP

Wing Commander D.K.L. McDonnell
RAF Brize Norton

A British Airways Jumbo Jet was cruising along at 33,000 feet on its way to New York when the controller said:

"Speedbird 43 climb immediately to 35,000 feet for noise abatement."

The crew of the Jumbo looked at each other in amazement for, even though pilots are well used to minimum noise climbouts from airports, it was the first that any of them had heard of a noise abatement climb 6 miles high; so they queried it:

"London Control; confirm the climb to 35,000 feet is for Speedbird 43 and is for noise abatement?"

The London controller confirmed the requirement, a little testily, so the aircraft duly climbed. Meanwhile the crew had taken the opportunity to check all of their procedure manuals, but could find nothing to suggest why a noise abatement procedure should be initiated at their height. So they queried it once again:

"London Control this is Speedbird 43. Please give reason for noise abatement climb; we can find no procedure."

"Roger," replied the controller, "have you ever heard the noise two Jumbos make hitting each other?"

Flying Officer D. Tomaney
RAF Shawbury

☆ ☆ ☆

An American tourist in Paris, visiting Notre Dame, was enchanted by the depth and beauty of the bellringing in the famous cathedral. Deciding to take a closer look, he climbed the steps to the top of the spire, to be greeted by the grotesque figure of Quasimodo, the hunchback of Notre Dame.

"Gee, Quasi," gushed the tourist, "your music sure is swell. Could you play me another tune?"

"Yes Master," croaked the hunchback, and shuffled off towards the largest of the bells. Curiously, instead of using a rope, he pushed the mighty instrument away from him with his great strength and, when it swung back, met it full on with his forehead. The bell emitted the richest, deepest sound imaginable.

"Say, that is wonderful!" exclaimed our tourist, "can I have a go?"

Quasimodo seemed reluctant to allow this but, sensing his admirer's enthusiasm, he beckoned the man closer. Positioning himself in the perfect place for maximum resonance the tourist met the swinging bell head-on. It emitted a barely audible "Ping" and, at the same time, catapulted our intrepid traveller out of the cathedral window. There was a sickening crunch as he hit the pavement far below.

At ground level, as a crowd gathered and a gendarme inspected the body, Quasimodo appeared at the bottom of the steps; he was looking very guilty. The gendarme turned the dead man over and asked the hunchback in an accusing voice: "Do you know this man?"

Quasimodo shuffled over to the messy scene, looked down and said:

"Nope. His face doesn't ring a bell."

Flight Lieutenant I.H. Stevens
RAF Personnel Management Centre, Innsworth

☆ ☆ ☆

During the evacuation of British nationals in the Indo-Pakistan war of 1971, a United Kingdom Mobile Air Movements (UKMAMS) team was tasked to fly with the RAF Hercules aircraft to several locations to pick up British nationals, mostly civilians. One such excursion was to Chaklala in Rawalpindi.

When the team arrived at the airfield they were met by a scene of some confusion; people were milling about everywhere, and some of them were very confused and frightened. Eventually the team made contact with the British

Embassy and the tedious task of "processing" all the passengers began. There was much argument about who was entitled to leave, and even more about which possessions could be taken on the aircraft and which had to be left behind. Eventually, however, the baggage was secured on the aircraft, the passenger list was agreed with the Embassy, and a Corporal from the UKMAMS team led the passengers out to the aircraft.

"Now let's be having you ladies and gents," he instructed in a Yorkshire accent, "move right to the front and sit down please, don't leave any gaps."

Shortly thereafter the aircraft was choc-a-bloc and, to give further instructions, the Corporal had to stand on the rail above the centre seats. From this vantage point he noticed a space in the seating.

"Come on now, ladies and gents; move up and don't leave any spaces."

At this, a young man in a white suit stood up next to the gap and started waving his arms at the Corporal.

"Having trouble with your seat belt are you, Sir?" shouted the Corporal above the babble, "I'll be there in a minute; just close up for now, please."

"No!no!" said the young man, "we need this seat."

"What for?" asked the agitated Corporal.

"We need a fourth for Bridge."

Sergeant Keith Parker
UKMAMS, RAF Lyneham

☆ ☆ ☆

Those of you who remember the Meteor aircraft – the RAF's first jet fighter – may recall that it could be a pig on single engined landings. If one allowed the speed to fall off too far, and got 'on the wrong side of the drag curve', there was just not enough controllable power available on the live engine to recover; result – usually a crash in the undershoot. It is a fact that the RAF lost more people practising this emergency than as a result of actual engine failures. Indeed, practice approaches with one engine shut down were eventually banned; the 'failed' engine thereafter had to be left at idling power.

On a training sortie in the 2-seater variant, before the ban was imposed, a student had made a number of 'hairy' approaches; the instructor each time having to take over and go round again to avoid becoming a smoking heap. His last attempt was as bad as ever, but this time, as the speed was falling off and getting near the critical value the student said:

"Shall I put some more power on, Sir?"

"No, sod it," said the instructor, "let's crash!"

Mr Peter J Lynn
General Manager, Marshalls of Cambridge, RAF Shawbury

Once upon a time, a farmer owned a large, handsome, ginger tom cat of which he and his children were very fond. As is not uncommon with the breed, his pet went on regular nightly prowls, returning the next morning looking somewhat bedraggled but clearly contented with life.

It soon became apparent, however, that these nightly forays were causing problems on neighbouring farms. Too often, unwanted litters of kittens were having to be put down, with the usual accompanying tears and tantrums from the other farmers' children. The colouring of the kittens involved left no doubt as to the villain of the piece, so a delegation from the neighbouring farms called on our farmer and issued an ultimatum: either get the tom seen to or keep him away from other farms – he would henceforth be shot on sight. Our man was fond of the cat so, faced with this risk, he reluctantly arranged to have it doctored.

Afterwards, he was somewhat surprised to find that the tom's nightly wanderings continued; so one night he decided to follow him to see what he got up to. The cat wandered off into a nearby wood and perched himself on a tree stump in a clearing. Before long, several other cats appeared – all toms and all undoctored – and the ginger tom started meowing and caterwauling while the others sat around.

The moral of the story was immediately obvious to the farmer: although one may be finished "operationally", one may still be useful in an advisory capacity!

Anon

☆ ☆ ☆

A Chief Petty Officer in the Womens Royal Naval Service (WRNS) was warning her girls about the imminent arrival in port of the US Fleet. She noticed one girl manicuring her nails and apparently not paying the slightest attention. She admonished the girl forcefully, reminding her of the number of Wrens who had been in trouble after the previous visit.

"I'll be all right," said the girl, tapping the side of her head, "I've got it up here."

"It doesn't matter where you've got it," replied the Chief Petty Officer, "them buggers will find it!"

Squadron Leader (Retired) M.J. Fletcher
RAF Linton-on-Ouse

☆ ☆ ☆

The Station Warrant Officer (SWO) is a revered and (in the case of junior airmen) feared figure on a RAF station. A mere summons from the SWO can usually be guaranteed to strike terror in the heart of most airmen, particularly if they do not know its purpose.

One day HRH The Duke of Edinburgh was due to visit our station and the Station Warrant Officer sent his newest and most junior airman, a Leading Aircraftman, to the main gate; he had strict instructions to inform the SWO as soon as the Duke arrived.

A large black car arrived, complete with star plate and pennant. The airman stopped the car and asked the passenger if he was The Duke of Edinburgh.

"No," replied the passenger, "I am Air Vice Marshal Brown, the Air Officer Commanding Number One Group." The airman thanked him, saluted, and let the car pass.

Shortly afterwards another car arrived, bedecked with star plate and flags. Again the airman asked was the passenger The Duke of Edinburgh.

"No," was the reply, "I am Air Chief Marshal Green, the Air Officer Commanding in Chief Strike Command." The airman duly saluted and waved this one on.

A third car arrived with even more decorations. The airman asked his question and, this time, the answer was in the affirmative.

"Well I should push off quickly if I were you," said the airman, "the SWO is after you!"

Wing Commander R. Sturman
RAF Brize Norton

☆ ☆ ☆

A ten year old boy came home from Sunday School. "Tell me, what did you learn today?" asked his father.

"Well," said the boy, "we had this really brilliant story; it was about this Israeli General called Moses. He was leading his armoured column in a retreat from Egypt after a surprise attack. The Egyptian army was in hot pursuit and, although Moses kept calling in air strikes upon them, they were gaining rapidly on the Israeli column. Then the reconnaissance squadron radioed in with another problem; the Red Sea was ahead of them and blocking their escape to Israel. Moses sent a signal to his static headquarters, and they despatched a team of combat engineers, who managed to build a pontoon bridge across the Red Sea just before the Israeli armoured column arrived."

"As the leading Israeli tanks started across the bridge, the leading Egyptian tanks were only a couple of miles behind the Israeli rearguard, and gaining rapidly. So Moses called in a flight of F4 Phantom fighter-bombers with laser-guided bombs. The Phantoms attacked the bridge, and destroyed it just before the first Egyptian tanks reached the far side. All the Egyptian tanks were sunk with the bridge and the Israelis escaped."

"Are you sure that's the way the story went?" asked his father, looking extremely doubtful.

"Well, not exactly," said the boy, "but the way *they* told it, you would never have believed it."

Group Captain J.K. Walters
Commanding Officer, RAF Church Fenton

☆ ☆ ☆

A man was recently arrested in downtown Lincoln at 2am, stark naked. When asked by the police to account for his actions, he described how a young yuppie couple had just moved into his local village to capitalise on the house price differential between there and London, where the couple both worked.

"They threw this party to make the locals feel that they were being neighbourly," said the now shivering man to the very doubtful looking policeman. "Well, some time after midnight, the husband turned all the lights off and said that all the ladies should take their clothes off. When the lights went on, sure enough, all the ladies were in the nude. Then, a bit later, he turned the lights off again and said that all the men should take their clothes off also. And, sure enough, as the lights came on, all the men were in the nude. Then the husband said 'OK lads, go to town!'... And... well... I seem to be the first one here, Officer."

Group Captain T.G. Thorn, AFC MRAes
Headquarters RAF Support Command

UPSIDE DOWN . . .

☆ ☆ ☆

The story is told of how Queen Mary was somewhat apprehensive when King George V went down in a submarine for the first time. She is said to have remarked "I shall be most disappointed if he does not come up again".

The Most Reverend and Right Honourable Dr J.S. Habgood
The Lord Archbishop of York

☆ ☆ ☆

There once was a man who was anxious to get rid of his wife. As she was totally unwilling to give him a divorce, and in any case he could not face the financial strain of supporting her for the rest of her life, he sought the services of a "hit man" in the local area.

His furtive enquiries led to the suggestion that he should go to a pub called The Eagle, and negotiate with a man called Arty. At their subsequent meeting Arty agreed to do the dastardly deed for the sum of one pound. The husband told Arty that his wife worked at the local Tesco supermarket, where she usually finished work at 5.30pm.

On the appointed day the hit man, briefed by the husband that the wife would be wearing a yellow coat and red wellingtons, positioned himself outside the supermarket just before 5.30. A woman fitting the description emerged and the villain lured her round to the back service entrance and strangled her. As he was leaving the scene, apparently unnoticed, Arty saw to his horror that another woman had just left the supermarket, also wearing a yellow coat and red wellingtons. Rather that risk his reputation, he repeated the process with her and again escaped. However, he had been seen on this occasion, and was arrested shortly afterwards.

The local paper ran the story the next day under the headline:

ARTY CHOKES TWO FOR A POUND AT TESCOS.

Wing Commander P.T.W. Leaning
RAF Brize Norton

☆ ☆ ☆

A Yorkshireman travelling on the overnight train from Paris to Lille, was awakened by the young mademoiselle occupying the upper bunk complaining of the cold.

"Would you like us to act as man and wife?" he asked.

"Oui, oui, monsieur," she replied.

"In that case, you can get your own blanket!"

Councillor J.L. Carter
The Lord Mayor of Leeds

☆ ☆ ☆

A senior police officer was travelling to a meeting at the Home Office when, to his dismay, he noticed that his watch had stopped. It was important that he should arrive at the meeting promptly, so he used his car radio to ask Scotland Yard for a time check.

In response to this enquiry from an unfamiliar callsign, the strident voice of the female radio operator asked him what Force he was from.

"Of what possible relevance is that," he retorted.

"Oh, it's very important," came the reply, "if you are from the Met, it's 1200 hours; if you are with the Kent Constabulary, it's 12 o'clock, or lunchtime. For the Dorset Force, both hands are on the 12; and if you come from Avon and Somerset, it's Wednesday!"

Anonymous
RAFPMC

☆ ☆ ☆

Back in the days when the Cold War was at its height, the crew of a RAF transport aircraft carried the Prime Minister to Moscow for a Summit. Having disgorged the official party, the crew were driven down town and checked in to a very sumptuous (by Moscow standards) hotel.

As they were settling down for the night the Captain heard a knocking at his bedroom door. Opening it, he found the co-pilot standing outside with a worried expression on his face. "I wonder if I could have a private word with you in my room, Sir?" he asked.

The Captain followed him to the other room. "What on earth is the matter?" he asked once they were inside. The co-pilot put his finger to his lips and silently beckoned him into the bathroom. Once inside, the co-pilot turned the bath and shower taps on full blast and flushed the toilet noisily in the best James Bond tradition. He put his mouth against the

Captain's ear and whispered: "You remember the security briefing that we were given?"

"Yes."

"You remember they warned us that the KGB would almost certainly try to compromise us, and that our rooms might be bugged?"

"Yes."

Leaving the background noise running, the co-pilot led the Captain back into the bedroom and pointed silently under the bed. Right under the centre of the bed there was a small bulge in the carpet. As quietly as possible the two men lifted and moved the bed; they rolled back the carpet equally silently to reveal a metal knob protruding from the floorboards. After experimenting for some time, the men found that it appeared to be screwed down, and started very gently turning it in an anticlockwise direction. Eventually it came free but, to their horror, there was a deafening crash from the ballroom below as the chandelier crashed to the floor!

Anon

☆ ☆ ☆

A honeymoon couple were preparing for their first night of nuptial bliss. The bridegroom took off his trousers, handed them to his wife, and instructed her to put them on. Needless to say, they were far too large for her; the waistband of the trousers almost reached her neckline.

"I can't wear these," she said, handing them back.

"So just remember that," he replied, "in this household there is only one person who can wear the trousers."

He went off to the bathroom, smiling to himself. When he returned to the bedroom, his bride was in bed with the covers demurely pulled up under her chin. She smiled enticingly and pointed to a pair of her silk panties laying at the bottom of the coverlet.

"Why don't you put those on before you join me," she purred.

Eager with anticipation, he pulled them over his ankles but found that he could not get them past his knees.

"I'm afraid I can't get into these," he said, looking crestfallen.

"No," she replied, "and you never will unless your attitude changes!"

Group Captain R.J. Wharmby
Commanding Officer, RAF Chivenor

☆ ☆ ☆

Following an engine failure, a RAF pilot ejected from his crippled aircraft. As advertised, the automatic mechanisms in the ejector seat caused him to be separated from the seat and deployed the parachute. However, at this stage the pilot realised that something did not feel quite right and, looking up, he saw to his horror that the parachute rigging lines were badly twisted; this had reduced the effective area of the parachute canopy to about half its normal value. He realised that this would increase his rate of descent to a dangerous, if not fatal, extent.

He spent some time vainly trying to recall what his parachute training had taught him to do in these circumstances before resigning himself to an uncertain fate. Suddenly he sensed movement beneath him and, looking down, observed something flying up towards him from the ground. It turned out to be a man wearing blue overalls, carrying a spanner, and with no visible means of support. As the man approached the pilot, polite to the last, said:

"Excuse me, but do you know anything about parachutes?"

"No," said the man, "and precious little about gas stoves!"

Air Vice Marshal M.J. Pilkington, CBE
Air Officer Commanding Training Units, Headquarters RAF Support Command

During the winter of 1978 there was a period of over a week when North Devon was isolated from civilisation by heavy snow. The only way in or out was by helicopter, and then it was that the Search and Rescue Whirlwind helicopters of RAF Chivenor came into their own. The crews were working 24 hours a day carrying relief food supplies, and transporting patients to hospitals – everything from emergency accident victims to mothers-to-be.

On one of these many hospital runs a helicopter, with five patients on board became what the navigator fraternity call "temporarily uncertain of position"; in plain English – lost.

There was some excuse; the snow obscured all ground markings. The roads were distinguishable only by the tops of the telegraph poles, and there was only one railway line in the area. Over such ground and in such weather, it would have been unwise to attempt to put the helicopter down so, to resolve the "uncertainty" it was decided to lower the helicopter winchman down to a road sign outside a small village, to discover exactly where they were.

To the unconcealed amazement of the five patients, the helicopter door was opened and the winchman clipped himself to the cable; he launched himself into space and disappeared into a cloud of blowing snow. Those still in the helicopter caught occasional fleeting glimpses of him as he reached the ground and brushed away the snow obscuring the sign. He then gave the signal to be winched up again.

The navigator, who was also the winch operator, could hardly wait for the winchman to re-enter the cabin before asking excitedly:

"What did it say, what did it say?"

"It said," replied the winchman between gasps, "Please drive slowly through the village!"

Squadron Leader J. Whitehead
RAF Chivenor

☆ ☆ ☆

An elderly Jew was walking through a park; as he passed an ornamental lake, he heard a small voice say:

"Please kiss me, and I will turn into a beautiful Princess and we will live happily ever after."

He looked around, but could see nobody. The plea was repeated several times before he identified the source – a small frog sitting on a stone in the lake. The Jew picked up the frog, put it into a box and walked on.

"Why won't you kiss me and let me turn into a Princess?" came a small muffled voice from the box.

"Princesses are ten a penny," he replied, "but with a talking frog... Oy vey... have we got something."

Mrs M. Beaumont
RAF Church Fenton

☆ ☆ ☆

A wealthy Northern businessman, down in London for a two-day conference, ended up in a West End nightclub on his own. During the course of the evening he fell into conversation with an attractive young lady. It emerged that she was a chorus girl "resting between engagements" and, after several drinks, she agreed to spend the night with him for the sum of £500. She accepted that he could not produce that sort of money in cash and did not have his chequebook with him. He undertook to send her a cheque immediately he returned to work; to maintain discretion, he would have his secretary post the cheque which would apparently cover his temporary rental of a London apartment.

Back in the North again, he began to have second thoughts about whether the experience had been worth the sum agreed. He asked his secretary to post a cheque for £250, covered by the following letter:

Dear Madam,

Please find enclosed a cheque for £250 for the rental on your flat. You will note that it falls short of the amount originally agreed. However, at the time agreement was reached, I was under the impression:

a. That it had never been occupied.

b. That there was plenty of heat.

c. That it was small.

In the event, I found that it had been previously occupied; there was little heat – if any – and it was altogether too big for my comfort.

Yours faithfully . . .

The reply came by return of post:

Dear Sir,

I cannot understand how you could have expected a desirable property to have remained unoccupied. As for the heat, there is plenty – if you know how to turn it on. On the question of size, it can hardly be my fault that you did not have enough furniture to fill it.

Yours faithfully . . .

SAC D.G. Norvill
RAF Chivenor

☆ ☆ ☆

On several occasions during the early 1980s I was detached to the British Forces in Belize, Central America, as a Puma helicopter pilot. One St Patrick's Day morning my crewman and I had been working in support of the Irish Guards who were stationed in the South of the country. Much to our amusement, we had been briefed that our flying programme would encompass a visit to every outstation and patrol that the Irish Guards had out on the ground that day. Ostensibly, this was for the usual ration and water resupply but, in reality, it was for a very different reason – at each location we were to hand out bunches of shamrock so that each soldier of the regiment could wear "The Green" in his hat on this special regimental day.

The morning's sorties proceeded much as planned. Sweaty, grimy faces emerged from various jungle clearings and grinned as we handed out the shamrocks. We wondered how many of the ration packs contained a bottle of the "Hard Stuff". After three hours flying we were about half way through our day's work, and it was time to head back to the main garrison base at Rideau for lunch.

As we walked into the camp it was apparent that the Regimental Sergeant Major had organised several "field days" during the last week. The camp usually had the unmistakable stamp of a regiment of the Household Division but, on this particular day, it was immaculate. The entire garrison had been paraded on the square in the muggy heat of the Belizean midday sun.

Hastily skirting the parade ground, trying not to make the place look untidy, we met a fellow aviator coming in the opposite direction. It was Staff Sergeant B*****, an Army Air Corps pilot who was well known to us from other theatres of operation – we had last served together in Rhodesia.

"Cor, have you ever seen anything like it?" he said after exchanging pleasantries. "What a load of f***ing craphats!"

The Staff Sergeant, being a "Corps-man", was not very fond of regimental tradition. After indulging in the usual aviators' banter and generally denigrating a fairly impressive parade, he bade us farewell and proceeded on his way.

From the welcome shade of a nearby Atap hut we made ourselves comfortable and watched the parade. There would be no lunch until all the ceremonial had ceased, so we might as well enjoy it. As the guardsmen wheeled, saluted and perspired in the sun we could see, in the background, Staff Sergeant B***** walking around the outside of his Scout helicopter.

With the parade at the halt the Battalion Commander addressed his troops. His words have long been forgotten, but he did comment on the very special efforts that had gone into making this a memorable day; "The Greens" had been flown out from England and delivered to all soldiers of the Regiment, no matter where their location. Finally, he was proud to announce that their Colonel-in-Chief had graciously recorded a message for the Regiment and that without further ado they would now all listen to it before retiring for lunch. In the muggy midday heat the stillness was broken only by the occasional raucous call from a nearby tropical bird. Not a muscle moved on the square as the Colonel leant forward and pressed the button of the tape recorder on a nearby table.

"My Irish Guards..." began the clear and unmistakable tones of the Queen's voice.

Suddenly, faintly at first but slowly gathering volume like some alien banshee, the rising tone of a helicopter engine shattered the tranquillity and completely obliterated Her Majesty's address. Stoically, the guardsmen remained motionless in their positions. The muscles in the Colonel's cheeks clenched as the clatter of the rotor blades built up to an ear-shattering crescendo. Staff Sergeant B***** went slowly, carefully and meticulously through his pre-flight control checks, functional checks and take-off checks. A cloud of dust drifted towards the parade, covering the guardsmen and their highly polished accoutrements with a gritty film. With a deepening roar, the helicopter lifted off into the bright blue Belizean sky.

As the whirr of the rotors faded into the distance, the serene Royal voice could again be heard, delivering the concluding remarks:

"... next year at Windsor Castle."

Squadron Leader P.Q. Hallett
Headquarters Strike Command

An Air Traffic Controller, having completed three years at RAF Gutersloh in Germany, was posted to RAF Wyton in Cambridgeshire. A few days after his arrival there, he was given an inbound transport aircraft to control. Having identified the aircraft on his radar, he said: "RAFAIR 710 you are identified ten miles North of Gutersloh." Almost immediately he recognised his mistake and said: "RAFAIR 710, correction, you are identified ten miles North of Wyton."

"Too late for apologies," replied the pilot, "I have just shot my navigator."

Flight Lieutenant P.C. Dyer
RAF Shawbury

The student pilot on the University Air Squadron had not had a good day. Through sheer incompetence he had crashed and destroyed one of the Squadron's few and valuable aircraft. On the other hand, he had emerged from the mangled wreckage largely in one piece.

UPSIDE DOWN . . .

The usual crowd of onlookers had gathered round the wreckage, where the Very Mature Engineering Manager (VMEM) of the contractor who serviced the Squadron's aircraft was working out what, if anything to do with the heap of metal.

"Was the pilot hurt?" asked one of the onlookers.

"No," replied the VMEM, they wouldn't let me near the little bastard."

Mr H.G. Highmore
Chief Engineering Manager, Marshalls of Cambridge, RAF Shawbury

A young mother was determined that her husband should play a part in caring for their first-born.

She instructed him to bathe the child but was aghast to discover him holding the child by the ears, swishing him to and fro through the bath water.

"That is not the way to bathe a child," she cried.

"Yes it is," he replied, "when the water is as hot as this."

Air Vice Marshal R.M. Austin, AFC
Air Officer Commanding and Commandant, Royal Air Force College Cranwell

☆ ☆ ☆

Whilst being sworn in for what promised to be a lengthy trial, a juror asked if he might be excused on the grounds that his wife was due to conceive the next day. At this point the clerk to the court rose to explain to the judge:

"I think the gentleman means that his wife is due to be confined, M'lud."

"The difference is immaterial," replied the learned judge, "for whichever of you is right about the exact nature of the event, his presence is clearly essential!"

Squadron Leader C.E. Vary
Headquarters RAF Support Command

☆ ☆ ☆

A young lady went to see her doctor with what she described as a most embarrassing problem.

"I am an air hostess," she said, "and, as you will appreciate, I have to bend over the passengers in the aisle seats in order to serve those sitting next to the windows. My problem is that I suffer rather badly from flatulence, so that every time I bend over, I pass wind. Fortunately for me, it is always absolutely silent and odourless – but *I* know that it is happening and it is giving me a complex."

"Well that is a new one on me," said the doctor, "are you sure that it happens *every* time?"

"Oh yes," she affirmed, "I just bend over like this and... there, it happened again.... no external clues, but I am absolutely mortified."

"Well," said the doctor, "I am going to give you some yellow pills. I want you to take two after each meal, three times daily for a week, and then come to see me again."

A week later she was back in the office. "You have made it worse," she stammered, blushing; "not only does it still happen, but now it makes a distinctly audible noise."

"I am encouraged to hear that," said the doctor. "We seem to have cured your ears; now let's think what we can do about your nose!"

Anon

☆ ☆ ☆

A VC10 transport aircraft of the RAF was tasked to collect a British Army unit from a training area in Kenya and bring them back to the UK. The Army detachment commander, a very officious major, had managed to alienate the entire flight crew during the preparations for departure. He seemed to quieten down once the aircraft taxied but, as soon as it had reached cruise altitude, he attempted to attract the attention of the Flight Sergeant Air Loadmaster.

"Staff Sergeant, Staff Sergeant," he shouted down the aisle. The loadmaster ignored him until a soldier touched him on the shoulder and pointed towards the gesticulating major.

"I'm sorry, Sir," said the loadmaster, "but actually, I'm a Flight Sergeant."

"Well, if you were in the Army, you would be a Staff Sergeant."

"Wrong," said the loadmaster, "if I were in the Army, I would be a Lieutenant Colonel!"

Squadron Leader L.R. Powell
RAF Finningley

☆ ☆ ☆

A fisherman who had been fishing for most of the day had caught nothing. He was about to give up when his luck changed and he landed a salmon parr. Although too small to weigh in, the fisherman decided he would place the parr in his keepnet; at least he had caught something. He decided to stay a little longer and cast his line into the river once more and settled down.

"Please put me back into the water," he heard a quiet voice say. The fisherman looked round but could see no-one. Again he heard "Please put me back into the water." He could hardly believe his ears but it was the fish that was talking to him.

"I can't put you back again," he said "you are my catch for the day. Besides I can't believe you can talk!"

"Oh I can talk alright and my name's Rusty. Now you must put me back into the water. I have a lot of living to do and many oceans to visit. My life is just beginning. Please, please put me back into the water."

After a while the fisherman could see he was not going to catch any more fish and gave in. He put the salmon back into the water and went home.

Some five years later the fisherman was fishing in the same spot when he got an enormous bite and after a lengthy battle, landed a mature salmon weighing some 10 lbs. He unhooked the fish and put it in his keepnet.

"Hello again," a voice said "do you remember me?"

"Rusty?" asked the fisherman.

"Yes," said Rusty, "and let me tell you that have I had the most marvellous time since we last met. I have visited almost every sea and ocean and have seen some wonderful sights. Why I have even seen the Titanic. What a ship. I was inspired so much that I have written some poems about it."

"You're pulling my leg," said the fisherman.

"No I'm not," said Rusty. "In fact I have even had the poems published. You may know the title 'Titanic Verses' by Salmon Rusty."

Sergeant M.R. James
RAF Church Fenton

☆ ☆ ☆

A very old house, in Ireland, was being taken apart brick by brick by a gang of Irish navvys. During this exercise, the gang discovered a priesthole wherein lay a skeleton.

The police were called and the skeleton was taken away for examination. After a number of days, the police were able to identify the skeleton from dental records as one Shamus O'Flaherty whose home town had been Dublin.

Further investigation revealed that in his day he had been a famous celebrity; he had been none other than the 1923 all Ireland hide-and-seek champion.

Sergeant M.R. James
RAF Church Fenton

☆ ☆ ☆

A considerable amount of RAF squadron training takes place overseas. The popularity of the locations varies. Some are warm sunny places – the sort that other sections of the population choose for holidays; others are cold, isolated and miserable.

A front-line Tornado squadron had just returned from one of the former places where they had been accommodated very close to a well known and rather expensive holiday resort. The squadron commander's joy at his reunion with his family was rather tempered by the news that his Station Commander wished to see him immediately. On contacting this worthy, he was told to don his best uniform immediately and proceed to the Commander-in-Chief's office for a "hats on" interview; there was no clue as to the purpose.

Very shortly thereafter, the squadron commander was standing at attention in front of a very stern looking CinC who said:

"Wing Commander; it has been drawn to my attention that Buckingham Palace has recently received a postcard from your squadron, thanking Her Majesty for sending you away to such a lovely place with so much sun to continue your training. The Palace authorities are not amused; and neither is the Ministry of Defence. Such behaviour is puerile, reprehensible, and brings the good name of the Service into disrepute. I hold you, as squadron commander, personally responsible for this faux pas. Before I decide how to deal with the matter, have you anything to say for yourself?"

A pregnant pause ensued as the chastened Wing Commander searched for a reply. Finally, he looked the CinC in the eyes and said:

"Before I reply to that, Sir, do you happen to know whether the Prime Minister's postcard ever arrived?"

Wing Commander S.J. Mawson
RAF Sealand

At an Officers' Mess Ladies Guest Night the rather large wife of a senior officer developed a severe case of flatulence.

On each embarrassing occasion a young officer nearby – her husband's Aide de Camp – apologised to the assembly.

A visiting American officer, seated in the same area of the dining room, was full of admiration for the young officer's courage and gentlemanly conduct in attempting to take the blame. Towards the end of the dinner, while a distinguished guest was speaking, the blushing lady was overcome by a particularly severe spasm. The dining room fell silent, and the gallant junior officer squirmed under the stare of all the onlookers. The American officer beamed over the top of a large cigar and said in a cool Texan drawl:

"Say, lady – why don't you have that one on me?"

Wing Commander D.C. Bernard
RAF Stafford

☆ ☆ ☆

Early in his flying career, a young student was offered the chance of night flying with his instructor. He seized the opportunity as this was a new experience for him. As they were flying along, admiring the lights below, he began to wonder what would happen if something went wrong.

"Sir, what would our actions be if we had an emergency?" asked the student in a timid voice.

"Perform the immediate actions drill and deal with the emergency," came the reply.

"What would you do if you needed to force land?" the student asked.

"Complete the forced landing checks and glide towards what looks to be a clear area. On the descent, do your pre-landing checks and switch on the landing lamp close to the ground..and, if you like what you see, land".

"What if you don't like what you see?"

The instructor gave the student a compassionate look in the dim cockpit and said.

"Turn the landing light off!"

Officer Cadet O.B. Whyatt
RAF Cranwell

☆ ☆ ☆

St Peter was at the Pearly Gates when a man in Flight Lieutenant's uniform wandered up looking somewhat puzzled.

"Are you really an RAF flight lieutenant?" asked St Peter.

"No, I'm just a university graduate doing basic flying training," he replied. "My parents live in a flat in Swindon, and I had been home for the weekend. My car was parked outside, and before driving back to Cranwell I looked up and waved goodbye to Mum. That's the last thing I remember."

A short while later St Peter was surprised to see a man in a Wing Commander's uniform.

"Are you a real Wing Commander?" asked St Peter.

"No, I'm afraid I'm just the Station Dentist at RAF Brize Norton," he replied. "I've recently moved into an upstairs flat in Swindon. The lady next door phoned to ask if I had any spare sugar, so I took a cupful round to her. She kindly offered me a cup of coffee, and we were sitting having a chat when we heard somebody entering the flat. The lady became very agitated and told me to hide. The refrigerator was empty so she pushed me in and shut the door. After that, everything is a blank."

A short time later a very irate man wearing a Squadron Leader's uniform reported to St Peter.

"Are you a real Squadron Leader?" asked St Peter.

"No, I'm a VC 10 captain," he replied. "I was scheduled to do the Far East run, but due to the lousy weather the trip was cancelled and I went home. When I got into the flat the wife was looking very guilty, and there were two cups of coffee on the table. I had a quick look round, and happened to glance out of the window. Down below was a young man just getting into his car. He looked up, grinned at me, and gave me a wave. In an attempt to disable his car and stop him getting away, I tipped our old unserviceable refrigerator over the low windowsill. Unfortunately, due to the wind and rain I lost my footing and fell out after it!"

Squadron Leader C. Richardson
RAF Cranwell

A panda was becoming very bored, sitting in his cage in a zoo. He began chatting to the monkey next door. The monkey suggested that he might like to go over the wall one night and pop down town, where he would find a couple of good pubs and clubs. That night, the panda escaped from the zoo, went into town and settled himself into the first pub he found. After a while, he found himself chatting to a very attractive young lady. Over the course of the evening, he bought her a considerable number of drinks and some quite expensive snacks – smoked salmon sandwiches, caviar and the like. She mentioned in the course of conversation that she was a prostitute but the panda, an innocent abroad, did not understand the term. When she eventually invited him to accompany her home, he was overwhelmed, and lost interest in what the unfamiliar term might mean.

Back at the young lady's flat, the panda had an experience of a lifetime; and it lasted all night. He awoke, somewhat exhausted, in the morning and was leaving to return to the zoo when the young lady said:

"Excuse me, aren't you forgetting something?"

"I'm sorry, I don't understand," he replied.

"I'm a prostitute," said the young lady, "look it up in the dictionary."

Opening the book at the appropriate page he read: "Prostitute: a woman; demands money in return for indiscriminate sexual favours."

"Ah, I see," said the panda as realisation dawned. He handed back the dictionary, saying:

"Well, I'm a panda; look that up."

The young lady opened the book and read... "Panda: A black and white bear from China. Eats shoots and leaves".

No 5 Flight
No 122 IOTC, RAF Cranwell

During the last war the crew of a Mosquito were shot down in rough country to the South of Murmansk and floated to earth on their parachutes. The temperature was 25 degrees below zero; they had been on patrol for a long time and were feeling fairly low as they landed in the outback with no visible signs of civilisation. After a couple of hours, as they trudged wearily towards the West, they looked up to see that they were confronted by a large brown bear. The navigator, realising that his last day had come, dropped to his knees and started to pray. The pilot on the other hand, dropped his survival pack to the ground, pulled out a pair of running shoes and started to put them on. The navigator turned to him in disbelief.

"Good God man," he said, "what are you doing? You know that you will never outrun the big brown bear."

"I am aware of that," replied the pilot, "but all I've got to do is to outrun you!"

Group Captain T.E.L. Jarron
Commanding Officer, RAF Cranwell

A retired drill instructor, now a Chelsea Pensioner, was admitted to a Royal Air Force hospital for specialist treatment by the Consultant Advisor in Dermatology. The day after his admission the hospital was honoured with a visit from the Queen. Prior to the visit, there were the predictable panics and worries and the Matron visited each patient to remind them of the protocol if Her Majesty spoke to them.

The Royal Visit progressed well until the Queen entered the old drill instructor's ward. Learning that he was a Chelsea Pensioner, Her Majesty went straight to his bedside and began talking to him. The Matron was beaming, and the Commanding Officer was delighted to find a patient of his arousing such interest. The old drill instructor lay rigidly at attention in his bed and answered each question in staccato fashion.

"And what are you in here for?" asked the Queen.

"I've got boils on my bum, Ma'am," he responded.

The Matron had an apoplectic fit and the Commanding Officer quickly started to move the Queen on. A little later, the old man was given a severe talking to about the more basic aspects of Royal protocol.

The following day an officer was admitted to the same ward. He was an RAF flying instructor; in fact he had taught Prince Charles to fly, and had remained a friend of the Royal Family. A few days later, Prince Charles arrived out of the blue to visit his friend. The Commanding Officer was summoned hastily and arrived in a panic with the Matron in tow just as Prince Charles moved from his friend's bed to engage the Chelsea Pensioner in conversation.

"How are you today?" asked the Prince.

With the Commanding Officer and the Matron both glaring at him, the old man replied:

"The skin infection on my back is clearing up nicely, Sir, thank you."

Matron beamed; the Commanding Officer sighed with relief.

"Oh, that's good," smiled the Prince, "the boils on your bum have cleared up then!"

Squadron Leader S. Blackburn, MBE
Headquarters British Forces Cyprus

☆ ☆ ☆

An elephant inadvertently wandered into a swamp in Africa and started to sink. His cries for help were heard by an eagle, who swooped down to investigate and perched in a tree at the edge of the swamp.

"Please help me, Mr Eagle," called the elephant, "I am sinking fast and will soon drown."

"I don't see that there is much I can do," said the eagle; "I can lift moderately heavy prey off dry ground, but picking up an elephant that is already embedded in a swamp is, to be brutally frank, quite beyond me."

"Well please see if you can fetch some help – quickly, I implore you," shrieked the elephant.

The eagle flew off at high speed. The first person he found was a lion who was polishing his Porsche 944 Turbo outside his den.

"Quick, Mr Lion," said the eagle, "our friend Mr Elephant is sinking in a swamp and will soon drown if we don't help him."

"Very unfortunate," said the lion, "but I don't see what I can do about it. King of the Jungle I may be; but hauling elephants out of swamps is hardly my forte."

"But there must be something we can do to help," sobbed the eagle; "what about your car – could you tow him out with that?"

"I suppose we could try."

The lion and the eagle arrived back at the swamp in the Porsche in record time. The lion attached his tow rope to the back of the car; the eagle carried the other end of the rope over the elephant and dropped it to him. The elephant grasped the rope with his trunk; the lion gave the Porsche all 212 brake horsepower and, very slowly, the elephant was pulled out of the swamp to safety.

Some weeks later, the eagle misjudged a swoop on to a small animal and found himself sinking in the same swamp. His cries for help were heard by the same elephant.

"Sorry mate," said the elephant, "I've been in there once, and I know that I could not help at all."

"Well please go and get Mr Lion and his car," shrieked the eagle, "and for God's sake be quick."

"Sorry again," replied the elephant, "but Mr Lion drove off on his holidays this morning – he's off to live it up in the South of France."

"Surely you can do something," begged the eagle, "after all, I was instrumental in saving your life the other week."

"OK," said the elephant, "I certainly owe you my life; but this is really going to hurt me." He took his appendage and swung it over the swamp; the end landed about a foot from the eagle's head. The eagle clamped his beak onto it and the elephant, trumpeting with pain, walked slowly backwards. Accompanied by loud squelching noises, the eagle was pulled to safety.

The moral of this story is that, if you have an appendage like an elephant, you don't need a Porsche to pull the birds!

Squadron Leader P. Bristow
RAF Church Fenton

☆ ☆ ☆

It was the afternoon of the annual Royal graduation at the Royal Military Academy, Sandhurst. The weather was fine, the Queen had just taken the salute, and the whole assembly was waiting for the traditional climax to the ceremony, where the parade adjutant was to ride his horse up the imposing steps of the main Academy building and into the Great Hall.

Horse and rider set off up the steps but, about half way up, the horse suffered a severe bout of flatulence, the noise of which reverberated all round the parade square.

Immediately after the parade had dispersed the mortified adjutant sought out the Commanding General to express his sincere apologies.

"I'm so embarrassed, Sir," stammered the red faced sub-altern. "It could not have happened on a worse occasion, what with the Queen being there and everything. But there was just nothing I could do about it."

"Don't worry about it, old chap," said the General sooth-ingly, "most people thought it was the horse."

Pilot Officer N. Cairns
RAF Finningley

☆ ☆ ☆

My grandfather was one of the longest living Yorkshiremen in history. He ascribed his incredible longevity to his habit of eating a dessertspoonful of gunpowder after breakfast every morning of his life. When he eventually died at the age of 126 he left:

6 children
17 grandchildren
51 great grandchildren
108 great great grandchildren

and an emormous smoking crater where the crematorium used to be.

Anon

☆ ☆ ☆

A senior RAF officer was stopped by a police patrol car on the motorway one evening.

"Excuse me, Sir," said the policeman through the driver's window, "but would you mind stepping out of the vehicle and accompanying me to the rear?"

The officer obliged but, when they reached the rear of the car, he burst into tears.

"Oh my God," he shrieked, "what a disaster. How on earth will I explain it to my wife? She will kill me; I'll never hear the last of it!"

"Come, come now, Sir," said the policeman soothingly; "it's not that serious. It's only a rear light bulb; even on a brand new Volvo it will only cost a few pounds to replace. I'm sure your wife will understand."

"Never mind the bulb," screamed our hero, "where's the bloody caravan?!"

Wing Commander R. Springett
RAF Stafford

The new Station Medical Officer was doing his first inspection of the Junior Ranks Mess and was appalled at the poor hygiene standards he saw. The cooks' clothing was filthy, they had long hair and dirty nails, they served food with their fingers whilst smoking on the servery, and the kitchen was a shambles. He gave the head chef 14 days to sort the place out under threat of a posting to Machrihanish if he failed.

A fortnight later the doctor returned to find the place transformed. The kitchen sparkled, the cooks were immaculate and each had their own set of serving tools on a belt round their waist. The duty cook on the servery politely asked an airman what he wanted and, taking his tongs, carefully served a mixed grill. To the next he served a portion of roast chicken and to another a grilled steak, carefully using the tongs to place the food on the plate. The doctor was very impressed and complimented the cook on his hygienic practices.

Whilst chatting, the medical officer noticed a piece of tape sticking out of the cook's trousers. When asked what it was for, the cook explained:

"Well sir, the chef is very hygiene conscious, so now when I want to go to the toilet I don't have to use my hands because I just pull on the tape and the deed is done."

"Excellent," said the doctor, "but what happens when you've finished?"

"Ah well," replied the cook, "you see these tongs ..."

Flight Lieutenant D.I. Rudd
RAF Valley

☆ ☆ ☆

The Mastermind contestant was approaching the end of his specialist round on "Famous Speeches of the Second World War".

"Who said: 'We shall fight on the beaches'?"

"Winston Churchill, London, 4th June 1940."

"Who said:" (the buzzer sounded) "I've started, so I'll finish. Who said: 'I shall return'?"

"General Douglas MacArthur, The Philippines."

"And at the end of that round, Mr Gordon, you have scored 14 points. You passed on only one: 'What the bloody hell was that' was said by Emperor Hirohito, Hiroshima, 6th August 1945."

Group Captain (Retired) John McDonald
Associated Aircraft

In the days when we had proper aircraft carriers, and before they angled the flight decks and such like, the approach to the ship was guided by a "batsman". He would stand at the side of the flight deck, carrying what looked like a pair of table tennis bats; with these he would give signals to the approaching pilots to guide them to a safe landing.

Every Navy pilot was expected to become competent at this type of approach, but obviously it was too much to expect them to try it for the first time on a real flight deck. Initially they had to practise on a large airfield – with room for error – before moving on to an aircraft carrier for 24 carrier landings to complete their training. The preparatory training at an airfield was known as Aerodrome Dummy Deck Landings – ADDLs for short.

There was one Australian pilot, very short of stature, who had a lot of trouble with his ADDLs, and was considered barely competent to move on to the real carrier; but barely competent *is* competent, so off he went. His first passes at the deck were frightening in the extreme, and he was "waved off" a number of times before he eventually managed a sort

UPSIDE DOWN . . .

of controlled crash on to the flight deck. He was immediately summoned before Commander (Air), who conducted a very one sided interview:

"What the hell do you think you are up to? You don't appear to be taking any notice of the batsman's signals; can you see him?"

"Not very well, Sir."

"What position do you have your seat in?"

"Fully down, Sir."

"Well of course you can't see properly then, you short arsed little runt. There is a lever alongside your seat; pull it and put the seat right up – then perhaps you won't kill yourself."

As he paused for breath at this point, the Australian said:

"Oo's goin' to work the bleedin' rudders, then?"

Mr P.J. Lynn
General Manager, Marshalls of Cambridge, RAF Shawbury

The Commandant of the RAF Fire School was somewhat worried when he received an irate telephone call from a nearby farmer. Air pollution is a fairly topical and emotive subject these days, so the farmer's claim that the dark pall of smoke from a practice fire had engulfed his workers and caused work to be suspended, had to be taken seriously.

The Commandant was naturally concerned and asked when the incident had occurred, how many workers had been involved, and what sort of work was being held up.

"It's happening now," said the farmer, "I'm calling from the field on a portable 'phone. There's only three farm hands involved, but the trouble is we cannot see our hands in front of our faces to control our stubble burning!"

Wing Commander A.J. Gritten
RAF Manston

☆ ☆ ☆

A group of trainee multi-engined aircraft pilots at RAF Finningley were renowned for reporting even the most trivial of in-flight occurrences. After one particular sortie the student pilot entered in the After Flight Log:

"Unfamiliar noise from port engine".

After several fruitless hours of examination, and having found no apparent fault, the engineer tasked with the rectification entered in his job sheet:

"Engine run for 4 hours. Noise now familiar!"

Student Officer P.M. Williamson
RAF Cranwell

☆ ☆ ☆

Some years ago I was in a recruiting appointment which involved lectures and interviews at all kinds of obscure locations. One evening I was parking my car in a rough part of town when I was approached by a couple of scruffy looking youths aged about 12. They drew my attention to the area's reputation for crime, and offered to "look after" the car for me for a small sum of money.

Recognising this as a juvenile protection racket, I told them to get lost; I also pointed out that I had left my Alsatian dog in the car, and woe betide anyone who might think of interfering with it.

"Oh yeah?" sneered the larger of the two, "What's he like at fighting fires, then?"

I paid!

Flight Lieutenant (Retired) A.F. Carter
Bromley

☆ ☆ ☆

A young Jewish couple, after six months of marriage, went to see their doctor because they had failed to start a family.

"How often do you make love?" asked the doctor.

"Make love?" queried the young man, innocently.

"Well, what do you do when you go to bed at night?" the doctor continued.

"Oh. We kiss each other and go to sleep said the young wife.

"Then I will have to show you what is required," said the doctor. He asked the wife to remove her clothes and proceeded to demonstrate the technique in great detail.

"And that," said the doctor breathlessly, "is what is required; at least twice a week."

"Fine," said the husband, "I could bring her in on Mondays and Thursdays.

Wing Commander S.G. Griffiths
RAF Linton-on-Ouse

☆ ☆ ☆

Three young boys were fishing in a canal by the side of a road when a large car skidded off the road and plunged into the water. They ran to the sinking car and helped the occupants to escape. To their amazement, one of those they had rescued turned out to be the Prime Minister.

"Thank you so much," said the PM, "You must allow me to reward you for such bravery. There must be something that I could give you; what would you like?"

"I would very much like a new BMX bike," said the first boy.

"You shall have one tomorrow," said the PM.

"Do you think I could have a computer?" asked the second boy.

"Certainly," said the PM; then, turning to the third, "And how about you?"

"I should like a state funeral," said the last, glumly, "because when my father finds out who I've saved, he'll kill me!"

Squadron Leader C.R. Gilding
RAF Church Fenton

☆ ☆ ☆

An American WASP society hostess found herself short of six male guests for a very important reception. She rang the Commanding General of the local Army training unit to ask if he would send six of his best young men to make the numbers up. "But no Jews," she insisted, "I'm sure you will understand."

At the appointed hour, the doorbell rang and the butler showed in six negro cadets. The hostess immediately rang the General's number again, but could only reach his secretary.

"There must be some mistake," said the hostess, horrified.

"Oh no, Ma'am," said the secretary, "General Cohen never makes mistakes."

Wing Commander S.G. Griffiths
RAF Linton-on-Ouse

☆ ☆ ☆

It was approaching the end of the war in the Pacific and the Japanese realised, at last, that it was beginning to look as if they might lose. At this stage a notice was placed in Station Routine Orders at every station of the Imperial Japanese Air Force; it asked for volunteer aircrew to take part in unspecified special missions.

Some three weeks later, several hundred volunteers, covering the entire rank spectrum, were assembled on a Pacific airbase to be briefed by a General. A hush fell on the briefing room as the General entered.

"Good morning, gentlemen," said the General. "I am sure that you must all realise that the war has not been going well for us recently. The special mission that you have all volunteered for will change that picture entirely and will allow us to defeat the Western imperialists for all time. It will regain the honour of Nippon and of the glorious Emperor Hirohito."

He reached to the table beside him and removed a cloth covering a model aircraft. It was slim and sleek with a long nose and short, stubby wings.

"This," continued the General, "is our new secret weapon, and you glorious sons of Nippon are the ones who will fly it. It is very fast and has a long range; in fact the main American Imperialist fleet, which is out of range of other aircraft based here, can be attacked from here with this aircraft – and with fuel to spare."

"Starting tomorrow morning, I will be launching you in flights of six in these aircraft, which we have called "Divine Wind". Each flight leader will take his team up to 20,000 feet and head West; after about two hours flying – the exact figures will be given tomorrow - you should gain visual contact with the American fleet, far below and looking like model ships on a painted ocean. The flight leader will designate individual targets for each aircraft, which will than dive towards its target with full power selected. Now you can see the reason for the sleek lines of this aircraft for, in this power dive, it will achieve speeds well in excess of 400 knots; thus it will be virtually impossible for the filthy imperialists to intercept it with other aircraft or to engage it with anti-aircraft fire."

"As each of you approach your designated target, you should manoeuvre so as to keep the black cross in the centre of the windscreen over the bridge of the ship to be attacked, and hold it there until impact. Now you can see why the aircraft has such a long nose; in this nose, in front of the pilot, is 3000 pounds of TNT with an impact fuse. As you hit the ship it will detonate and destroy the ship entirely. By this time next week, we should have destroyed the entire Western naval presence and, effectively, we shall have won the war for the Emperor. Now, gentlemen; are there any questions?"

Right at the back of the briefing room, a diminutive Japanese Second Lieutenant rose to his feet and bowed three times towards the General.

"Yes Sir, General," he said, "I have a question. Are you out of your f***ing mind?"

Captain R.H. Stalker
Monarch Airlines

☆ ☆ ☆

During the Second World War a new Army recruit attended his first dance at a unit with a joint Army/Royal Air Force population. He found himself dancing with a young lady in a brown uniform, with whom he felt he was making something of a hit.

"Look, I'm a bit new to this setup," he said, "what does that WRAC on your uniform stand for?"

"In your case," said the young lady in a knowing way, "WRAC stands for 'a walk round and a cuddle' – if you're lucky, that is."

"Oh!" said the recruit, "in that case I think I'll go and look for one of those WRAF!"

Group Captain R.E. Williams
Commanding Officer, RAF Swinderby

☆ ☆ ☆

A pilot walked into the Station Medical Centre one morning covered in cuts and bruises; he asked for an appointment with the Medical Officer.

"What on earth has happened to you?" asked the doctor.

"One of my wife's nightmares," replied the pilot.

"Gets a bit physical in bed then, does she?" enquired the doctor with a nudge and a wink.

"Not in the least," he replied, "she talks in her sleep. Last night she woke up screaming 'Get out quickly, my husband's coming'. Like a fool, I leapt out of bed and jumped out of the window."

Flight Lieutenant N.J.B. Brown
RAF Marham

☆ ☆ ☆

Whilst on vacation in New England a career girl from New York discovered, for the first time, the latest fad amongst food freaks. She found Scrod, a species of fish which originated in Boston, to be absolutely delicious.

On returning to New York she learned in conversation that the delicacy could be obtained in certain restaurants in that city, and determined to experience it again. She was given the name of a restaurant just off 42nd Street, whose Scrod had been widely acclaimed, and arranged to take a girl friend along to try it.

When they hailed a New York cab, she found herself a little vague on what the exact name of the restaurant was, and indeed on exactly in which street it was situated. After a long and rather fruitless conversation with an increasingly irritated cab driver, she eventually said:

"Look, you know New York; you know the area we want to be in. We just want a place where we can get Scrod."

UPSIDE DOWN . . .

"Lady," said the cab driver, "I've been asked that question a lot of times in my business; but dat's de foist time I ever hoid it in de plupoifect subjunctive!"

The Honourable Alan Clark, MP
Minister of State for Defence Procurement

☆ ☆ ☆

In the beginning was The Report, and then came The Assumptions. The Assumptions were without form and void, and The Report was without substance.

And darkness was upon the faces of the workers; and they spake unto their Flight Commanders saying "Verily, it is a crock of sh** and it stinketh."

And the Flight Commanders went unto their Commanding Officers and sayeth unto them "It is a pail of dung and none may abide the odour thereof."

Whereupon the Commanding Officers went unto their Air Officers Commanding and sayeth unto them "It is a vessel of fertiliser and none may abide its strength."

So the Air Officers Commanding went nigh unto their Commanders in Chief and sayeth unto them "It contains that which aideth plant growth and it is very strong."

And the Commanders in Chief went unto the Chief of the Air Staff and sayeth unto him "It promoteth growth and is very powerful."

And the Chief of the Air Staff was mindful of what was told unto him and went unto the Minister saying "This powerful new initiative will promote the development and efficiency of the Service; yea verily I say unto you that it shall be as cold water to the thirsty soul and is recommended with all my heart.''

And the Minister looked upon The Report and he saw that it was good. And The Report was made Policy.

Flight Sergeant O. Turner
RAF Odiham

☆ ☆ ☆

A recently retired Army officer answered an advertisement in The Times for an assistant manager's post at The Savoy Hotel in London. At the subsequent interview, the manager stressed the importance of smartness, punctuality and tact in whoever was selected for the job.

''Well,'' said the officer, ''my Service background naturally makes me smart and punctual, but what the hell is tact?''

''Let me give you an example,'' said the manager. ''This morning the tea boy went sick, so I had to take the morning tea myself to all the rooms that had ordered it. I came to one room where I could hear the sound of the shower running when I knocked and received no reply. I knocked again without response then, after a third knock, I used my pass key and entered. I was confronted by an open shower, with no curtains drawn, and a beautiful young lady taking a shower therein.''

''Good heavens,'' said the officer, ''what on earth did you do?''

''Well, that is where the tact came in,'' said the manager; ''I went straight over to the shower, placed the tea on a shelf, said 'Good Morning, Sir, and left; thus I avoided all embarrassment. Get the idea?''

"Brilliant," said the Army officer, "I'm sure I will get the hang of it."

"Right," said the manager, "we will take you on for a week's probation."

Three days later the probationer met the manager in the foyer and was asked how he was getting on.

"Fine thanks," he said. "That tea boy went sick again this morning and I had to take the tea round. When I got to the honeymoon suite there was a lot of banging and rustling of sheets as I knocked. After knocking three times without response I entered with the pass key and found a couple hard at it in the four-poster."

"Oh no!" said the manager, "what did you do?"

"Ah," said the officer, "I remembered your little tip. I went straight over to the bed, put the tea on the side table, tapped one of them on the shoulder and said 'Excuse me, but do either of you *gentlemen* take sugar?'"

Wing Commander N.M. Macleod
RAF Odiham

☆ ☆ ☆

One April day in 1927 a breathless secretary burst into the office of her tycoon boss.

"Sir, we have just heard that a man has flown the Atlantic; and, oh Sir, all by himself!"

"Miss Blenkinsop," said the tycoon calmly, "man by himself can do anything. When a committee flies the Atlantic, I should like to hear about it."

Squadron Leader R.W. Tizard
RAF Odiham

☆ ☆ ☆

President Gorbachev went into a hairdresser accompanied by two large bodyguards and asked for a haircut.

"Now Comrade President," said the barber once Mr Gorbachev was comfortably seated in the chair, "how is Perestroika going in the Soviet Union?"

The President said nothing; the barber continued with the haircut.

"Tell me President Gorbachev," said the barber a little later, "does Perestroika mean that I will be able to get a car more quickly?" Still there was no reply; the hairdresser continued to snip away.

"Please Mr President," said the barber after another pause, "will Perestroika improve the conditions of ordinary people in the Soviet Union?"

Can't you see," said one of the bodyguards, tapping the hairdresser on the shoulder, "that the President does not wish to talk?"

"That's all right," said the barber, "I don't want an answer; it's just that every time I mention Perestoika the hairs on his head stand on end and I find them easier to cut."

Air Marshal Sir Michael Graydon, KCB CBE
Air Officer Commanding-in-Chief, RAF Support Command

A Royal Navy officer serving at a Royal Air Force station attended a formal dinner for the first time since his attachment had started. He arrived in the ante-room for pre-dinner drinks and ordered a pint of bitter. As he did so a rather embarrassed silence fell on the assembled company.

"A beer?" queried the Station Commander, holding a sherry glass delicately between his fingers; "young man, it is a tradition in the RAF to drink sherry before a Mess dinner."

The Navy officer picked up his pint, swallowed the froth, wiped his mouth and looked the Group Captain straight in the eyes.

"Tradition, tradition," he exclaimed, "the RAF is not old enough to have traditions; that is a habit, and a very bad one!"

Wing Commander N.M. Macleod
RAF Odiham

☆ ☆ ☆

During an interview, ex-President Nixon was asked what he believed to be the soundest advice he received while in office. After a pause for thought he replied:

"I think the best advice I ever received came following the Watergate affair. One day I was being pursued through the corridors of the White House by FBI agents when an aide shouted: 'Run for the Oval Office, they can't corner you in there.'"

Group Captain J.C. French
Station Commander, RAF Odiham

☆ ☆ ☆

Once upon a time, in a far off jungle, there was a large tree which spread its branches both high and wide; it was the home of a tribe of monkeys and was known as "The Tree of Life"

The monkeys were born at the foot of the tree and, as soon as they were able, would climb to find a safe foothold on the lowest branches. As they grew older and stronger they would begin to climb further and further up the tree, fighting each other to establish a hold on each branch as they progressed. As they made their way upwards, they could see more and more monkeys struggling beneath them. The higher they climbed, the more furious the struggle for position became until one monkey would finally reach the single highest branch and look down in supreme triumph at the rest of the tribe.

The moral of this story is simple. As the monkeys struggled up the tree, they took pride in their progress, scorning those who struggled beneath them. What they tended to forget was that all the monkeys below them could see was a load of a***holes.

Squadron Leader D. Burley
RAF Finningley

☆ ☆ ☆

A Royal Air Force VIP transport aircraft of No 32 Squadron is ready for departure from Brussels international airport. The passengers include Ministers and very senior military officers, fresh from a NATO meeting. The weather conditions for the departure are expected to be turbulent. The stewardess, a tall, striking redhead, serves the VIPs with drinks and nuts as they board. As the aircraft approaches the take-off point, the stewardess says to the principle Minister:

"Excuse me Sir, may I take your glass as we are about to take off?"

"Do you mind if I hang on to it?" says the Minister, "I haven't quite finished it."

"That's perfectly all right Sir," says the stewardess, "but can you hold onto it very tightly as the take off will be bumpy; you had better hold onto your nuts as well."

No 32 Squadron
RAF Northolt

☆ ☆ ☆

An American Colonel from the deep South is on his way to a planning conference in Washington when he realises that he has forgotten some important papers. He hauls off the freeway into a service station, grabs a telephone, and hastily dials his home number. It is answered quickly:

"Yas'm."

"Is that you, girl?"

"Yas'm Boss."

"Git me the lady of the house."

"Ah caint do that Boss."

"Jest fetch her, girl."

"Ah caint; she'm indisposed right now."

"Cut the crap, girl; what's goin' on?"

"Ah got to tell you, Boss, she got a man upstairs."

"Whut? Now lissen, girl."

"Yas'm, Boss."

"Here's what you gotta do."

"Yas'm."

"You go to mah desk and git mah pearl handled Colt. You git upstairs and you shoot 'em both."

"Ah caint do dat, Boss."

"Girl; DO IT, do you heah me now?"

He hears the telephone placed on the table and, after a while, two muffled bangs; the breathless maid comes back on the telephone.

"Ah's done it, Boss. Ah's killed 'em daid. Ah don't know whut made me do it; must of bin de commandin' tone of yo' voice."

"You did good, girl."

"Whut shall Ah do with de bodies, Boss?"

"The hell I care; throw 'em in the swimming pool."

"But Boss, we doesn't has a swimming pool."

"Er... Umm... Is this Georgia 79314?"

Squadron Leader K.J. Lawry
RAF Benson

☆ ☆ ☆

An RAF delegation was visiting a South American country, where they were shown a large fish tank filled with piranha fish. In the middle of the tank was a large stone with an equally large diamond on top. Nobody, they were informed, had ever managed to extract the priceless diamond without being attacked by the piranhas and forced to give up.

Our heroes decided that this was too good a chance to miss, and drew lots for who should go first. The engineering officer won the first draw; he rolled up his sleeve, waited for a large gap to appear around the diamond, and plunged his hand in as quickly as possible. However, long before his hand reached the diamond, his arm had been eaten up to the elbow and he withdrew, hurt.

The second draw went to a navigator. He decided to be more scientific about it. With the aid of a hand held computer, a triangle and a stop watch, he worked out the angle of deflection, time on target etc; once he was satisfied, up went the sleeve and in went the hand. Alas, he also was too slow; his arm was eaten up to the wrist and he withdrew without getting near the diamond.

The administrator went third. He walked up to the tank, slowly and deliberately rolled up his sleeve, gently lowered his hand into the tank, and withdrew the diamond without a scratch upon him. His colleagues could not believe their eyes; until they saw the tattoo on his arm which read: *Administrators are the Greatest*. Apparently even piranhas will not swallow that!

Squadron Leader J.A. Edgell
RAF Benson

☆ ☆ ☆

Sex does three things for you: it makes you lose your memory ... I forget the other two!

Wing Commander D.M. Shannon
RAF Benson

☆ ☆ ☆

Seamus was injured in an industrial accident and received £25,000 compensation. After some consideration of what to do with his life and with the money, he decided to buy a smallholding and raise chickens.

Having bought a suitable smallholding, he visited the local livestock dealer and purchased a thousand day old chicks. Three days later, he returned and purchased a further thousand. When he subsequently returned for a third thousand, the dealer remarked that the business seemed to be thriving.

"Far from it," said Seamus, "Oi'm afraid the other chicks have all died."

"That's awful," said the dealer, "they were all very healthy chicks; what can have gone wrong?"

"To be sure Oi don't know," said Seamus plaintively, "Oi've been racking me brains over it. Do you think Oi might be planting them too close together?"

Wing Commander P.C. Dingwall
RAF Akrotiri

☆ ☆ ☆

What is the similarity between a Poll Tax collector, an ostrich and a flamingo?

They can all shove their bills up their backsides.

Group Captain D.H.A. Greenway, OBE ADC
Commanding Officer, RAF Benson

☆ ☆ ☆

A friend of mine was once posted to a RAF training school in the West of England, near to a large seaside town. The Station Commander at that time (the late 1970s) had many ideas for fostering good relations between the station and the local community; not all of these were popular with his staff.

The City Fathers were sufficiently impressed with the Public Relations emanating from the station to reward it by presenting it with a mascot, much to the delight of the Station Commander and the chagrin of some of his staff, including my friend. Being a seaside town, with a large expanse of sand, it seemed appropriate that the mascot should be a donkey. This creature is rarely depicted in military or aviation heraldry, and the image of a donkey representing an apprentice training school seemed rather ironic, if not insulting, to most of the station – but not, apparently, to the Station Commander.

Unfortunately this was not the end of the matter. The beast that was presented to the station by a grateful town (perhaps they were glad to be rid of it!) was not the demure animal often depicted as the humble beast of burden in the New Testament; neither was it a highly valued white donkey, much prized in the Middle East. Instead at the presentation a large, grey, evil looking male donkey (or Jack as they are known), smelling strongly of all those things that male donkeys smell of, lumbered forward and eyed the assembled Best Blue uniforms with a Gorgon's stare.

Now a live mascot, as many military units will know, needs considerable attention. This donkey was no exception; quarters were needed for it, and a handler was required. Fortunately a senior NCO from the Guardroom volunteered to look after 'Jack' and the two developed a remarkable affinity for one another. Why this should have been I do not know; they may well have shared the same RAF Education Test scores, or perhaps the donkey had been RAF Admin in a previous incarnation.

Having found a friend on the station, the donkey began to behave itself somewhat. From time to time it would forget itself and become excited; this usually manifested itself in the form of asthmatic braying whilst its penis extended as only a donkey's can. An apprentice was often employed to beat the animal's member with a pace stick in the hope that the donkey would concentrate its mind on something else.

As time passed, these minor failures in etiquette became rarer, and it was decided one summer's afternoon that the station mascot should be presented at a garden party in the grounds of the Station Commander's house; many civic guests from the local town were to be present.

All went well until the donkey, finding itself without its handler for some reason, decided to investigate its surroundings and stumbled in through the double doors leading from the garden into the house. Finding nothing of interest except a horrified steward, the animal did an about turn and dumped a large helping of manure on to the Station Commander's dining room carpet; it then trotted back out into the garden where it became once more – at least until the deed was reported – the focus of admiring attention from station management and guests alike.

There are perhaps several morals to this story, but I should like to leave you with just one: the locals are not always to be trusted!

Flight Lieutenant A.M. Bryne
RAF Church Fenton

During a break in an international convention, three men were discussing the meaning of the expression "savoir faire".

"Let me give you an illustration," said the American; "suppose that I returned home unexpectedly and found my wife in bed with her lover. If her first reaction was to say 'Good Evening darling' to me, *that* would be true savoir faire.''

''I disagree,'' said the Englishman, ''there needs to be a bit more to it than that. If I returned home and found my wife in bed with her lover, saying 'Good Evening darling' to me is no more than I would expect. But if she then turned to her lover and said 'Carry on my love', *that* would be true savoir faire.''

''No, no, no,'' exclaimed the Frenchman. ''Neither of you really understands the real meaning of the expression; only a Frenchman can grasp it. If I returned home and found my wife in bed with her lover, it would not surprise me if she said 'Good Evening darling' to me; nor if she then turned to him and said 'Carry on my love'. But if he was then *able* to continue, *that* would be *true* savoir faire!''

Air Commodore C.C.C. Coville
Headquarters RAF Support Command

☆ ☆ ☆

A Frenchman, an Englishman and an Irishman were marooned on an island. One day the Frenchman found an old lamp and rubbed it clean. As he did so, a genie appeared and granted each of the men one wish.

''I wish,'' said the Frenchman without hesitation ''to return to Paris, to my mistress.''

''If you please,'' said the Englishman, ''I should like to return to my own country also; to my country house and my family.''

The Irishman gave a broad smile. "I have so enjoyed your company and your conversation," he said to the others, "that I am going to remain here."

Marshal of the Royal Air Force Sir David Craig, GCB OBE DSc MA FRAeS
Chief of the Defence Staff

☆ ☆ ☆

An introduction to an after dinner speech which is more of substance than merely light hearted:
"It has been a busy time over the past few days. On Friday night I gave this speech at a nudist colony; on Saturday at a meeting of the Gay Liberation Front, and last night to Alcoholics Anonymous. For those of you now hearing it for the fourth time, I apologise..."

Air Commodore B.T. Sills
Air Attache, Bonn

☆ ☆ ☆

A new teacher, fresh from a South of England training college, arrived to start her first job in a Yorkshire village school. Walking into her classroom on the first day, she noticed a vase of dead flowers on her desk.
"Where do I get rid of these?" she asked one of the boys.
"In't bin Miss."
"I beg your pardon?"
"In't bin."

"Oh, I understand. In the dustbin. Now where do I find the dustbin?"

"I'nt yard."

She wandered out into the schoolyard, clutching the dead flowers and searching for the dustbin. Before she had found it, she saw the headmaster coming towards her and sought his assistance.

"Good morning Headmaster," she said brightly, "where's the bin?"

"I've bin to't privvy – not that it's any of thy business."

Alan Pedley Esq, DFC
Former Lord Mayor of Leeds

☆ ☆ ☆

There once was a multi-millionaire whose wealth had brought him everything a man could wish for – a country mansion, a beautiful wife, racehorses, the lot. One day, he returned from a three month solo safari to Kenya. As the chauffeur driven Rolls Royce carried him through the ornate gates at the end of his drive, the butler met him with a doleful expression on his face.

"What's the matter, Jeeves?" said the millionaire, winding his electric window down.

"I'm afraid that I have some very bad news for you, Sir," said Jeeves. "Your favourite dog, Reggie, is dead."

"How awful; how did it happen?"

"Your two million pound racehorse, Lucky Strike, Sir; kicked Reggie to death while in his own death throes."

"What? Lucky Strike dead as well; how come?"

"A beam from the stable roof fell on him, Sir; it was burning at the time."

"How on earth did the stable catch fire, Jeeves?"

"We think it was a stray spark from the fire at the main house, Sir."

"Oh no! The house burned down; how did it start?"

"The theory is that the wind blew the curtains on to the candles round her ladyship's coffin, Sir."

"My God! Angela is dead? What caused that?"

"Heart attack, Sir; when she heard the news that your company had crashed on the Stock Market."

"Jesus, Jeeves. It's the end of my world. Is there no good news at all?"

"Well, Sir," said the butler, looking a bit brighter, "what with the heat from the fire warming the ground, you have the earliest daffodils in Yorkshire."

Sergeant R. Miles
RAF Cranwell

☆ ☆ ☆

I was at table with a friend of mine on some important public occasion when he was due to make an important after dinner speech. The first course was a splendid hors d'oeuvre which he was obviously enjoying hugely. Suddenly there was a loud crack, and a look of consternation spread over his face. He had chewed with more enthusiasm than care on an olive which, unfortunately, had not been stoned.

"It's my false teeth," he said, "the bridge is broken." Just then the man sitting next to him said: "I've got a spare set; do see whether they fit."

They did; and my friend was able both to enjoy the rest of his meal and to give an excellent speech. When it was all over he surreptitiously slipped the teeth out of his mouth, wrapped them in a table napkin, and gave them back to the donor.

"Thank you so much," he said, "but how come you had them in your pocket? Are you a dentist?"

"No," said the other, "I'm an undertaker!"

Right Reverend David Konstant
The Bishop of Leeds